It's healing
and restoration
time. Seek God -
touch the hem of His
garment.

In His Service
Helen Noel

7 Days in the Fire

by

Helen D. Noel

authorHOUSE®

AuthorHouse™
1663 Liberty Drive, Suite 200
Bloomington, IN 47403
www.authorhouse.com
Phone: 1-800-839-8640

First published by AuthorHouse 2/26/2008

ISBN: 978-1-4343-4848-7 (sc)
ISBN: 978-1-4343-5930-8 (hc)

Library of Congress Control Number: 2007908375

Printed in the United States of America
Bloomington, Indiana

This book is printed on acid-free paper.

Italics throughout this book denote *"The Fruits of My Labor"* (*my childhood memories*). Names and titles of **God** are in bold Bernhard Modern font (including scripture) for the purpose of this book. In the name of **Jesus**, please do not read into the sentence structure of the names/titles.

A prayer for the reader:

Father, in the precious and mighty name of **Jesus**, as I read this book my prayer is that You will meet me where **I Am**. Speak healing and restoration into my past, present, and future. Please outstretch Your hand and give me a better understanding of my purpose through Your word, The Bible. **Holy Spirit**, give me ears to hear from You and the confidence and boldness to walk in Your way. Order my steps and help me to decrease so that You will increase. Fill my cup, **Lord** and grant me a greater illumination of Your promised eternal inheritance. Allow Your will to be done in my life. To **God** be the glory for all the things that He hath done. In **Jesus** name, Amen.

Your word is a lamp to my feet and a light for my path.
Psalm 119:105 (NIV)

CONTENTS

FOREWORD

This book is for anyone who has a soft and tender spot for family. Helen opens the windows of her heart and displays the many vessels that have made her the woman she is today. Although this book is from a personal account, the healing and restoration message is universal.

God inspired Helen to write *7 Days in the Fire*. At the heart of the book is a woman fighting for her life. During these "7" days of spiritual warfare, God unfolds pictures of her past, the significance of each day and visions of her future. Throughout her test, you will notice the love and concern that flowed in her home. Helen's faith in God provided her the strength and endurance to go through each day as she rehearsed generations of historical influences and present day Angels. Her perseverance from beginning to end motivates and encourages us to be strong.

This book captures the very handprint of God through family members, events, and even setbacks. Some events are painful, some will bring joy, but none-the-less, they are vital pieces of her story. You will recall people who sheltered you through words of wisdom, correction, and encouragement in the midst of your storm.

As Helen incorporates scripture in "He who has ears, let him hear," she provides the reader with nurturing fruit to increase faithfulness, purify hearts and offer them a different perspective on servanthood. The scripturally based essentials, if applied, will edify mind, body, and soul.

Family legacy and significant events (the little girl who pressed her grandmother's hair from the stove with a grease can and teakettle on top) shape and mold our character. Helen demonstrates that patience and forgiveness are critical character traits for Kingdom living. She emphasizes the need to "talk story" and embrace one another. This book makes you want to spend more quality time with your children; they too are a part of the generational fiber that binds us together in laughter, love and growth. You will be inspired to love deeper, help more and discover your purpose.

Bottom line, *7 Days in the Fire* is a road through the pages of the mind that will inspire you to go back down memory lane. It will motivate you to remain faithful to your established foundation. Life lessons become more vivid; stair steps to who we are today. It inspires you to tap into your God-given gifts and abilities that have been dormant for years. Not only will you see your past, but also you will embrace your future with an ever-present assurance that God's outstretched hand is always reaching out to you.

"It's wonderful to experience love unconditionally. Unconditional love is freedom from bondage."

Tawnya Kitt & Renee Lipscomb

ACKNOWLEDGMENTS

I praise God for using me as a vessel to write this book. I especially want to thank my loving husband, Irwin Noel, who stands beside me through thick and thin. His silent strength and faith carries our family through many storms. Our two sons, Tyrell (the firstborn) and Tavaris (the youngest) are miracles from You. My husband and I confess with our mouths and believe in our hearts that You set them apart to do great things. Thank You for Your outstretched hand of protection over our family. You have brought us through many fires.

I thank the Lord for preserving my parents, Charles Nelson, AKA Daddy, the patriarch of the Nelson family and Beatrice Nelson, AKA Mama, the matriarch of the Noel family. God has kept both of you in sound mind and body for such a time as this. The Bible says in Exodus 20:12 (NIV), "Honor your Father and your mother, so that you may live long in the land the Lord your God is giving you." I also thank God for my adopted parents, Columbus McGowan, AKA Mr. "G" and Mazie Wilson, AKA Ma Mazie.

I thank God for my spiritual parents, Bishop Mark Williams and Pastor Brenda Williams and for my entire church body at New Life Deliverance Temple where our motto is "Our church doors swing on the hinges of love." I thank Elder Alicia Pettus and Minister Annette King for coming to my house to pray for me the day I came out of the fire.

I praise God for my biological siblings: Yvette Miller, Tyrone Nelson, Debra Nelson, Vanessa Nelson, Algie Nelson, Rita Nelson, Benita Nelson, Renee Nelson, and my sister who went on to be with the Lord, Jacqueline Preston. Thank You for my other siblings: Tanya Douglass, Michelle Wright, Sharon Wright, Eric Wright, Ronald Wright, Regina Wright, Patrick Nelson, and Charles Nelson Jr. To my siblings who have passed away: Tambria Wright, Dwayne Henson, and Kent Nelson, we shall meet again. Our family ties will never be broken.

Praise God for my Wonderful Air Force-affiliated sisters-in-Christ: Twaina Carpenter, Tracey King, Audrey Clement, Tawnya Kitt, Myrna Miller, Melissa Lacey, Margo Miller, Robin Glover, Denise Tucker and Loretta Glenn. I thank my fellow Air Force Chief Master Sergeants-in-Christ for loaning me their ears: Bridget Howard, Renee Lipscomb, Carol Jackson, Edy Agee, Stephen Thomas and Anthony VanBuren. I thank God for my brother-in-Christ and spiritual advisor, Chief Master Sergeant Reginald Washington who went through the fire and nearly walked through the valley of the shadow of death before I finished this book. Your spiritual gift of prophecy kept me in expectation. I thank God for my Angels that covered me as I labored over this book: Pastor Alice Fagin, Pastor Cherelle Compton, Evangelist Carrie Johnson and her husband Erbert, Mary Helen Harding and Ellen Sawyer.

Thanks to my editors for loaning me their eyes: Robyn Endo, Jeanette Barrett-Stokes, Lillie Mello, Maisha Mello, Dede Haynes, Gail Lyons-Roberts, and Allyson Graham. Additionally, I would like to thank Kathy Mitchell, J.D. Compton and my photographer's Lorena Tejada Bell, Rhonda Schaefer and Larry Kirk. A special thanks to my niece Simone Nelson for researching information upon request.

Last, but certainly not least, I would like to thank my Air Force family and currently assigned squadron (Mission Support Squadron, "MSS" supports the best, yeah baby!).

DEDICATION

Dear Helen,

I love you very much. I'm glad you're my sister and friend. My earliest memories of you were as a **Teacher**. When I was four years old, you taught me to tie my shoes along with my ABCs and 123s. You used to read Tyrone, AKA Ty and I bedtime stories and played your flute to us. I remember when you and Ty made me fight our neighbor, Doretha. You said, "If you don't fight her back, I'm gonna' tell Mama and you're gonna' get a whoopin." As I grew older, you became an authority figure, my Mama #2. Your corrective eyes were always on me. I learned many foundational lessons from you, especially how to clean! I got upset when you made me re-do my chores because they didn't meet your standards. I thought I had to be perfect to gain your approval and if I wanted freedom I had to do things right, the first time. You were my example and role model for so many things. When you read from your red poetry book during your high school years, I didn't have a clue what the poems meant, but they sounded nice. You inspired me to write and I started a diary. I admired your closeness with your girlfriends. Remember the song by High Inergy, "You can't turn me off-not in the middle of turning me on"? Your dance group danced for hours as I watched from underneath the dining room table. I also loved watching you play basketball; I was so proud of you. I thought you were cool so I followed suit and played, too. I remember your AKA names, Queen of Hearts, Ms. Sophistication, and Sensitivity. You attended Civilian Conservation Corps when I was a teenager and

I was glad that we kept in touch. When you came home with Tito (the love of my life, smile), you showed me what a love-relationship looked like. You joined the military when I was 15 years old, but we stayed connected. I always looked forward to your return trips home. When I went to live with you in Las Vegas, we began new chapters in our lives. I felt like it was my rite of passage. Finally, I was old enough to hang out, go clubin', talk to men and be one of your girls. We had so much fun! During that time, you taught me how to take care of adult responsibilities. I learned another side of you and of life. In addition, I learned many valuable lessons, especially about men. You transformed from Mama #2, to my big sister and friend. It was a rough transition, but we made it! I've always looked to you for direction, inspiration and strength. In retrospect, you were Mama #2 because what you taught me had to be taught by you. Thank you for your interest in my development. You were a constant voice of wisdom in my head. I always wanted you to be proud of me. I've always cared what you thought of me and how I did things. You've been my inspiration and a role model for excellence. You instilled in me a high standard of achievement – "A 'nothing' is impossible mentality, you can do it, you're somebody - walk like it, talk like it, and live like it!" Continue to do what you do, the way you do it. Strive higher sister and I promise – I will meet you there.

I love you
Your baby sister, Yvette, AKA Vet

DEDICATION

My favorite cousin, Helen

You have always been special to me! I've been proud of you for as long as I can remember. We're closer than close and we've shared so much in our lifetime. You have always been a leader and I always followed you. I found myself in your shadow, wanting to do everything you did. Have you ever felt that way about me? We forever did things together and alike. It didn't matter if it was basketball, volleyball, or singing in choirs. I attempted to run track because of you (smile). I did what you wanted me to do, even if it meant I would get in trouble. Life is something; you never know what's in store. Many significant emotional events happened that caused me to change my thought process. I faced numerous trials and tribulations, many situations beyond imagination and control. My life changed drastically in November 1979 when Mama died. In all honesty, I didn't know how to handle it. I lost interest in everything good; the things we used to do were suddenly no more.

On May 10, 1983, as I suffered in the hospital through hard labor for twenty-two hours and reflected back over my life, I thought about the good, the bad and the ugly. Oh, how I wish my mother had been there to comfort me. I felt so alone. When you heard I was near delivery, you made a way to come see me. You'll never understand how precious that was to me. On May 12, you walked in the room with a big smile on your face and said, "Hey girl!" I was so elated to see you. Your voice and presence literally caused my baby to be born. Although they didn't allow you in the delivery room, we were together in **Spirit**; I felt your presence, right outside my door. It meant the world to have my favorite cousin with me, once again. You were the first family member to see my baby girl and chose her name, Tiana Rose. The day I entered motherhood, my life changed for the better. Prior to that day, I had lost my way, but my baby girl changed my focus point. When your life is full of hurt and confusion, you can't see your direction. Because of who you are, you redirected my thought process. It was as if you took my mother's place and I love you for that. I believe in my heart, had it not been for her death, I would have been more successful. You challenged me to do better and held me accountable. I remember when you said, "Angie, I don't know who you are any more." It hurt, but more importantly, it opened my eyes. Lovingly, you explained your words and made me love myself again, when I didn't want to. Your words penetrated my heart and soul; you made me understand life again. I watched you grow; you never stopped, never looked back, and never held anything back. You kept it real with a level head. We respect each other so much. There is nothing fake between you and me. I know you better than you know me and you know me better than I know myself.

Thanks cousin, I love you
Your favorite cousin, Angela Walls, AKA Angie

THE VISION

I received salvation on November 3, 1991 and shortly thereafter, the Holy Spirit began to reveal His omnipotent power to me. God said in Revelation 2:7 (NIV), "He who has an ear, let him hear what the Spirit says to the churches. To him who overcomes, I will give the right to eat from the tree of life, which is in the paradise of God." Speak Lord and I will always answer, "Yes, to Your will and to Your way."

Sixteen years ago, the Holy Spirit revealed that I had a book to write. As time passed, the Holy Spirit confirmed His revelation through Mama's words, "You walk with authority, with your head held high, as if you have a book on top of your head." After wrestling with my flesh for many years, I started writing about my childhood memories and entitled it *The Fruits of My Labor*. In expectation, I placed it on the shelf and patiently waited for the harvest.

From February 8 – 14, 2007, I didn't sleep for "seven" days straight, hence the title of this book, *7 Days in the Fire*. Biblically, the number "7" speaks of completion, perfection and rest. While in the fire, I rested in the shadow of the Almighty. On February 15, the last day of my trial, Satan tried to destroy me, but the Holy Spirit revealed, "Today is a day of significance, a day that will be etched in minds forever." I went to church for prayer and the Holy Spirit spoke the word "Mirror" through the minister.

My life flashed before me. **The Holy Spirit** revealed a vision of healing my body. On February 16, after a peaceful night of sleep, **the Holy Spirit** said, "Write" and He revealed another vision of a bride as I typed the "7" days of my warfare in one day.

As I typed, **the Holy Spirit** continually spoke "Bible" and He supernaturally renewed my mind, body, and spirit. *The Fruits of My Labor* symbolized the mind (childhood memories), the *7 Days in the Fire* symbolized the body (purging and deliverance) and **The Spirit** television station that I listened to as I typed symbolized **the Holy Spirit**.

While editing this book, **the Holy Spirit** revealed His also known as "AKA" names contained within. Names and titles of **God** are in bold print throughout the book. Names tell stories, describe, identify, and speak of reputation/history; they represent the very nature of a person.

Mama, you saw this book on top of my head many years ago and **God** birthed it for such a time as this. As I looked in the mirror of my past, **God** revealed the significance of each day as He connected the pieces to my past, present and future. The "Mirror" brought meaning to the phrase "You were made in **God**'s image." For the first time in my life, I saw myself made in the image of **God**. If you can see yourself made in His image, you too, will be able to see yourself in this book.

Chapter 1

MY GENESIS

The **Lord** is my shepherd; I shall not want. He maketh me to lie down in green pastures: He leadeth me beside the still waters. He restoreth my soul: He leadeth me in paths of righteousness for His name's sake. Yea, though I walk through the valley of the shadow of death, I will fear no evil: for thou art with me; thy rod and thy staff they comfort me. Thou preparest a table before me in the presence of mine enemies: thou anointest my head with oil; my cup runneth over. Surely goodness and mercy shall follow me all the days of my life: and I will dwell in the house of the **Lord** for ever. Psalm 23 (KJV)

According to John 1:1-5 (NIV), "In the beginning was **the Word**, and **the Word** was with **God**, and **the Word** was **God**. He was with **God** in the beginning. Through Him all things were made; without Him nothing was made that has been made. In Him was life, and that life was the light of men. The light shines in the darkness, but the darkness has not understood it." The family foundation was laid in the beginning.

My anointed and appointed grandmothers, Mommy and Mother Helen laid my spiritual foundation. **God** charged these

Angels to prepare **the Way** for me. Because of their faithfulness, His mighty hand of protection shelters me. I **A**m but one of their many seeds rooted and grounded in You. As I sat at Mommy's feet and lay in Mother Helen's bed, I was beside myself in **the Spirit.** As I stand on **the Rock**, I outstretch my hands to both of them. Their wisdom and gentleness lead me beside still waters. **God** ordered my steps because they walked steadfastly beside Him. My Angels taught me the beauty of life, how to plant seeds, and how to tend to the sheep. They taught me patience, to be still and to reap the harvest. In humility, they showed me how to enter His presence with thanksgiving in my heart and taught me that **Jehovah Jireh** is my provider. We are the blessings of Abraham. Through His seed, I've been fruitful and multiplied. I taste their goodness and smell their sweet aroma. They live through me; it's because of their obedience to **God** that I live. **Jesus**, I'm connected to You through the generational anointing. What a mighty **God** we serve!

The most deeply rooted seed my grandmothers planted in me was in accordance to Philippians 4:13 (NIV), "I can do all things through **Christ** who strengthens me." Many of my fondest childhood memories involved them. I was always cognizant of **the Holy Spirit** that hovered over my grandmothers. As I basked in their presence, I inhaled peace and serenity. **God**'s anointing flowed through them like streams of living water. During trials and tribulations, their legacies remind me that I **A**m more than a conqueror, the head and not the tail, above and not beneath.

I believe in the power of names. I was born Helen Nelson, the namesake of my paternal grandmother, Helen Nelson, AKA Mother Helen. **God** united me in marriage to a man with the same last name as my maternal grandmother, Hattie Noel, AKA Mommy. My **First and Last** names connect me to my grandmothers. My married name is Helen Noel. Helen means,

"Shining light" and Noel means "Christmas." My firstborn son remarked, "Shining light and Christmas" reminds me of "The Star of Bethlehem and The Birth of **Jesus**." There is power in the name, **Jesus**. Bear with me as I attempt to lay the foundation for these virtuous women - my praying grandmothers, Mommy and Mother Helen.

Mommy

My grandmother, Mommy was a petite Christian woman. Her husband, Chester Noel, AKA Papa died when I was three years old. Mommy's full name, Hattie Elena Viola Victoria Noel is memorable. Hattie means Home Ruler, Elena (a form of Helen "shining light"), Viola means flower and Victoria means victory. Her name suited her and she possessed an unfaded beauty of a gentle and quiet spirit. She was a woman of few words with a soft-spoken voice, slow to speak, slow to anger and quick to listen. Mommy always read her Bible. I had a praying grandmother.

*You considered her house your home, but you couldn't come as you were. Because of her holiness, before one entered her presence, they purified their mind, body and **Spirit**. You had to cleanse yourself from unrighteousness before your feet treaded on holy ground. As you walked through her house, you noticed hand-woven quilts, doilies and the plastic covered couch and chair in the off-limits sitting area. Her cleanliness was next to godliness with everything decent and in order. The soothing sound of gospel music filled the air. In her presence, because of His presence, there was fullness of joy.*

*Mommy's spirit reaped blessings and she had a disposition that resembled an Angel. **God** ordered her steps and I was drawn to her every move. Like a **Good Shepherd**, people flocked to her. She gave a good measure from her heart and never judged a soul. Mommy always kept a ball of folded dollar bills in a sock, tucked in her bra. Like a Good Samaritan, she gave money to the needy without expectation* of repayment. As a Christian, she knew her reward was in heaven because *Jesus* paid the price on Calvary.

Her profession was to serve others as a commercial cook in a nursing home. When cooking, she wore a checkered apron around her waist. Her ability to take a little and feed a lot seemed to parallel *Jesus'* miracle when He fed the multitude with two fish and five loaves of bread. The lingering smell of sweet pine-sol and home-cooked food filled every room of her house as it aroused my nostrils.

My grandmother's long hair symbolized her glory and authority; it was always neat with every strand in place. She consistently styled it in two braids, neatly tucked beneath her nape. Before bedtime, Mommy let her hair down to brush and comb it. She resembled an American-Indian. I watched in adoration as she washed her black, majestic, silk hair in the kitchen sink and then dried and straightened it.

I thought her hair was too beautiful to touch. One day, when I was twelve, I courageously asked her if I could straighten it. Surprisingly, she granted me the desire of my heart. Her love and compassion for me spoke volumes. I removed the chair from underneath the kitchen table and positioned it in front of the gas stove for her to sit in. Mommy handed me the Dixie Peach hair grease, a towel, and the straightening comb. I parted her hair in four sections, greased it, and placed the straightening comb on the "eye" (stove burner). I glanced at the permanently fixed teakettle and grease can on top of the stove. The aroma from the sizzling straightening comb filled the air.

Undeniably, I was nervous and excited. I looked at the hot comb on the eye and wondered, "What have I gotten myself into?" Mommy's spiritual gift in discerning of spirits sensed my reluctance as she humbly coached me through the process. I removed the comb from the eye, blew on it, rubbed both sides over the towel, and straightened the first section of her hair. She smiled patiently and we "talked story" (conversed/told stories). I asked Mommy to hold her ear before I straightened the *sides. The last thing I wanted to do was burn her ear. After I finished straightening it, she opened the drawer beside the stove, removed the hot curlers and then whispered, "Curl it too, baby." I had enough faith to move mountains and placed the curlers on the stove burner. When they were hot, I clicked them together and made the cutest little Shirley Temple curls in her hair.*

Mommy's hair was beautiful and so was she. I became her personal beautician and she paid me two dollars every time I styled it. The money was insignificant; I longed to make her more beautiful, by the touch of my hand. After I straightened and curled her hair, we found comfort in the living room where I sat on the floor in perfect serenity at her feet. She always wore ornamented slippers. The permanently attached Lazy Susan knick-knack on the center of her coffee table, aligned with my eyesight. Often times, we drank tea from her beautifully adorned teacups. Like in the Book of Colossians, Chapter 3 (NIV), Mommy was one of God's chosen people, holy and dearly loved, clothed with compassion, kindness, humility, gentleness and patience. She died on April 18, 1984 and Lord knows how much I miss her. I desire to sit at her feet and "talk story." Praise God, for my praying grandmother. Her legacy to me was a commitment to **the Spirit** of servanthood.

Family Vacation

Every summer we anticipated our family vacation to visit my other praying grandmother in Kansas City, Kansas. The night before our trip, we usually congregated in the kitchen to prepare convenient meals; some fried chicken, while others made bologna sandwiches and fixed kool-aid. We left early in the morning with what seemed like a million suitcases on top of the beige, green and brown station wagon. We feared the worst; within city limits the kids held their breath and slouched in their seats until we reached the highway. We were afraid that one of our friends might see us packed in the station wagon like sardines, as we resembled the Beverly Hillbillies.

The itty-bitty seat in the rear of the station wagon was my assigned seat; my little legs were scrunched the entire trip. Older siblings had privileges and being third from the youngest of ten had back seat written all over it. We looked forward to the gas and restroom breaks because it provided temporary relief from the confines of the station wagon. Upon arrival, we captured audiences as bystanders stared in disbelief. They were astonished by the number of people that one 1970-something Ford Country Squire could unload.

Mother Helen

My grandmother, Mother Helen, always heard our voices from inside the house and greeted us on the porch. She was an eloquent, short Christian woman with the strength of a giant. Like Solomon in the Bible, her wisdom captivated you through intellectual stimulation. Her formulated questions challenged you to think before you answered. I looked forward to the times when Mother Helen and I would "talk story."

She was also a woman of many sayings and she once referred to me as a "devil on wheels." Once while riding down the hill on my bicycle in front of her house, she began to look for me. I sped around the corner and she saw me and said, "There goes the devil on wheels." She rarely called me Helen, instead referred to me as "Namesake" or "Sunshine." The devil is a liar, and I knew she meant me no harm, but I preferred "Helen", "Namesake", or "Sunshine."

Mother Helen was a woman of servitude. Her talents included dressmaker, hat maker and beautician. Like Esther in the Bible, she carried herself like a queen and dressed to impress from head-to-toe. Her beauty treatments included facials, manicures, and pedicures. I admired her beautiful wardrobe and stylish hats stored in hatboxes throughout her bedroom. She had a beautiful fragrance of life like freshly picked lilies from a garden. Her expensive perfume bottles covered the vanity. Every year, I could hardly wait to sample each skillfully crafted fragrance.

Every summer, our family traditionally partook from Gates Barbeque in Kansas City because Daddy claimed it was the best in the world. He bragged about cream soda, too and we made special trips to purchase some. At night before bedtime, the grown-ups, as we referred to them, facilitated just-in-time sleep arrangements. I pretended not to hear them and continued to play with my baby doll. I always slept with Mother Helen; after all, I was her namesake. Every morning, I awakened to her sweet voice as it whispered, "Rise and shine, Sunshine" or "Good morning, Sunshine." I arose early to help her tend to the garden out back.

The sweltering summer heat shined brightly on us as we worked up a sweat in the garden. Sometimes, I prayed for soothing water or for rain to fall on us. I never complained about the heat because whenever I glanced at her, she smiled and continued to labor. We picked collard greens, turnips, beans, peppers and tomatoes or whatever harvest was in season. Mother Helen sowed and my family reaped her harvest. I especially loved the green tomatoes she fried for me.

On one occasion when Mother Helen and I "talked story" she revealed that the late Alex Haley, author of the Pulitzer Prize winning novel, "Roots: The Saga of an American Family" had eaten dinner at her house. She lived at 1315 Nebraska Avenue and Mr. Haley's brother lived several blocks away on Everett Street. Mother Helen's family lived in the house for over 64 years and preserved its rich history. When you entered Mother Helen's living room, the front-loaded wood stove with the chimney connector extending through the living room ceiling immediately caught your attention. Her passion for scrap booking and writing letters resulted in voluminous newspaper clippings being scattered throughout the house. As the family historian, she chronologically captured memories by writing on the back of pictures and traditionally enlightened me on the significance of remembering dates. Mother Helen died on October 13, 1995 and **Lord** knows how much I miss her. I desire to lie in her bed and "talk story." Praise **God** *for my praying grandmother.* Her legacy to me was a commitment to **the Spirit** of excellence.

I never knew her husband, my grandfather Algie Nelson, AKA Daddy Nelson. He died on January 7, 1960 before I was born. The 2007 Nelson Family Reunion revealed that he was head of his household, a kind and gentle man of God who made everyone feel important; no one burdened him. My cousin recalled a time when he made fermented grape juice and made-up a name for it, "Cha-wa-wa." Family members described him as a man of great dignity and integrity. Daddy Nelson emphasized education and I remember his brother's quote, "Whenever you say something, make sure you have something to say." Although he died before I was born, his legacy to me was a commitment to **the Spirit** of order.

HE WHO HAS EARS LET HIM HEAR:
Refer to the Bible, the Book of Genesis to gain a better understanding of your "Roots" and genealogy. You were created in the image of God. As children of God, we are Abraham's seed, heirs of the Kingdom according to the promise. We come from a proud heritage. **Jesus** is **the Root**, the foundation. There is power in the name, **Jesus** and He is **the Light of the World.** Somebody prayed for you and is praying for you. Don't be discouraged by what you didn't have, praise God for what you have. Seek God for wisdom and instruction and lean not on your own understanding. God kept you alive to fulfill your purpose.

Chapter 2

REST

FIRST DAY IN THE FIRE: Thursday, February 8, 2007

SCRIPTURE FOR THE DAY: Come to me, all you who are weary and burdened, and I will give you rest. Take my yoke upon you and learn from me, for I Am gentle and humble in heart, and you will find rest for your souls. For my yoke is easy and my burden is light.   Matthew 11:28-30 (NIV)

I have been on active duty in the United States Air Force for twenty-two years and God recently promoted me to Chief Master Sergeant, the highest enlisted rank in the Air Force. Generally, chiefs attend the majority of graduations and special events. On Wednesday, February "7", 2007, I attended an Airman Leadership School graduation and while there, I felt perfectly fine. However, as I drove off base, sickness entered my body. I considered a quick stop for medicine at a nearby convenient store, but decided against it. When I arrived home, my husband was in bed; I hurried out of my clothes, curled up my chilled body beside his and went to sleep.

9

The following morning, I woke up burdened with sickness in my body, and my soul cried out. From the moment I opened my eyes, I felt nauseous and could barely lift my head off the pillow. The pain felt like a smothering blanket pressing on my body that wouldn't let me breathe. I motioned my head to the right in expectation that my husband was still in bed, only to realize he had risen and was in the shower. I lay there alone with my eyes closed and felt the strongest urge to sleep. I needed to call my supervisor, so I outstretched my arm as far as I possibly could and fumbled to grab hold of the phone on the nightstand beside me. I told the Captain I was sick; he didn't recognize my voice. The devil stole it and I could barely speak. My body was so weak. I hurt from the crown of my head to the very soles of my feet. I knew that my mind, body and soul was under attack and I prayed to the **Lord** for shelter in the midst of this sudden storm.

During my pre-teen years, **God** *charged Ms. Mary, my Angel to protect me from the storms of life. She worked with Mama at the nursing home and her spirit was an ornament of grace. Ms. Mary took a special interest in me and I often wondered why she had chosen me. Occasionally, my Angel came by unannounced and asked if I could spend the night or weekend. Her house was a secret place to dwell, she showered me with agape love and spoiled me for no apparent reason. One year on my birthday, Ms. Mary gave me a beautiful white sweater as a gift. Whenever I wore it, I felt clothed in humility. I hid my love for it deep within my heart.*

Ms. Mary's love for me was like a hidden treasure. Every night before bedtime, she got on her knees, clasped both hands together and prayed and prayed and prayed. She prayed for everyone specifically by name, including me. I listened quietly as she prayed and sometimes, she sat me beside her and I prayed, too. My Angel taught me how to pray and to make my requests known unto **God***. We have not, because we ask not.*

The Captain asked if I needed someone to take me to the hospital and I replied, "No sir, I just need to rest." My husband walked into the room and saw me in the fetal position completely covered from head to toe. He asked how I felt; I uncovered my head and whispered, "I'm fine, I just need to rest." He placed his hand on my forehead, prayed, kissed me on the cheek, and left for work.

In my present suffering, I counted it all joy and rested in his prayer. The phone rang; I grabbled around the nightstand and finally took hold of it. My pregnant coworker who worked in the same office with me said, "Chief, I'm on my way to your house." I replied, "OK," then clicked the phone off and placed it on the pillow beside me. My body was too weak to return the phone to its base. As I wrestled with the pain, I felt like I needed to save every ounce of strength in me. I questioned if I had enough strength to answer the door, but chose not to worry. The joy of the **Lord** has always been my strength. I laid there and kept still.

I lay in bed as still as a mouse. My sons entered and asked if I was all right. I replied, "Mommy's sick." They loved on me, and proceeded to the bus stop in front of the house. I heard the keys dangle when my firstborn son locked the door. The devil stole my voice; however, **the Holy Spirit** sharpened my ability to hear and I heard every audible sound in the house. A few minutes passed and the familiar sound of keys startled me as someone unlocked the door for my pregnant Angel to enter.

The Angel entered and thanked my son for unlocking the door. She waddled in quietly and whispered, "Chief, are you alright? I'm here to take you to the hospital." I gently replied, "Not yet, right now I just need to rest." She asked, "Would you like something to drink?" I replied, "Yes" and she went to the kitchen. The cabinet doors clamored as she opened and closed them while she searched for a glass. She walked back into the room and handed me a glass

11

of orange juice. I asked her to wake me around nine o'clock. I yearned for sleep, but only rested. The fog grew heavier and heavier and I could barely see my way clear. I had no idea that I would be awake for the next "7" days straight.

At 9:00 a.m. my Angel stood over me and angelically whispered, "Chief, wake up, it's time to go." I was awake, but my mind was in a state of rest. I laid still a few minutes longer and prayed for strength. I got up slowly, pressed my way toward the closet and put on the first set of clothes in sight. After getting ready, I murmured to my Angel, "I'll drive myself." Shocked, she replied, "Are you sure, Chief? I can drive you." I held steadfast because I didn't want my illness to latch unto her body, especially since she was pregnant. I got in my car, and "physically" shook (to remove/ward off) my head, turned on some Christian music and prayed for favor all **the Way** to the hospital. I shouldn't have driven, but I had to protect the Angel **God** sent me. The 35 - 40 minute drive to the base seemed unbearable. **God** steered **the Way** as I followed behind my Angel's car and waved goodbye when we reached the hospital.

I walked slowly into the Emergency Room and a woman was standing at the counter conversing with the receptionist. I waited patiently and didn't complain. My eyes circled the room as I proceeded to the empty double chair against the wall. I longed for sleep, but only found rest. Minutes later, I formed a line and glanced at the woman standing at the counter. Her conversation seemed unimportant, but I kept my countenance because of the **Jesus** in me. She noticed me waiting and quickly departed. The receptionist asked for my identification card and for me to describe my symptoms. I passed her my identification and unexpectedly, she asked, "Did you bring your son in recently? I replied, "Yes." She smiled, and then said she recognized me and remembered my son. She told me to have a seat and someone would be with me shortly.

I curled up in the seat, after a few moments she called my name and directed me to section six. I sat on the bed, held my head down, took off my shoes and searched for a blanket to cover up, but none was in sight. I lay down and rested. A few minutes passed, the **Physician** walked in and asked what was wrong. I described my symptoms and he diagnosed me with an Upper Respiratory Illness, not infection, but illness. He took a throat culture, placed me on quarters (a medically authorized absence from work) for two days and prescribed medication. I walked slowly to the pharmacy.

At the pharmacy, I pulled the next ticket. There were hardly any empty chairs and I immediately thought, "I should have worn my uniform." Active duty personnel in uniform had priority. I was too sick to be concerned about who was present; I found a seat, curled up in it, closed my eyes and tried to take a nap. Eventually, I got my medicine and thought about the long drive home. I hung my head low, shook it back and forth and walked to the Admissions Office to turn in my quarters slip. The clerk must have felt my pain from the look on my face and said, "Chief, I'll fax your paperwork to your office, so you won't have to drive all **the Way** across base to deliver it." I didn't intend to drive across the base; home was my next stop. I smiled, thanked him, and then walked slowly to my car.

When I got in the car, I turned on some Christian music, shook my head and prayed for favor. I checked my voice mail and returned the Captain and a fellow Chief's call. Chief prayed for me and gave me a song, "Touched by His Spirit Divine." I experienced urges to vomit on **the Way** home. When I drove into my garage I said, "Thank you, **Jesus**." When inside, I went straight to bed with all my clothes on and covered myself completely from head to toe. Sporadic chills ran up and down my spine. I felt like something or somebody had taken their hand and pushed it through my flesh, wiggled it around my breastbone and pinched pieces of my heart. I was in pain physically, mentally and emotionally. I lay in bed caught between here and there; I couldn't sleep so I rested in the arms of **the Almighty**. I prayed for deliverance from the storm.

Later that afternoon, my sons came home from school and calmed the storm when they entered my bedroom. My firstborn kissed me and left. My "7" year-old son asked, "Do you want me to pray for you, Mommy?" I smiled and said, "Yes," pray on, my child. He placed his hand on my forehead, prayed for me and then said, "I hope **God** makes you feel better Mommy" and departed. At bedtime, I couldn't sleep and coughed all night.

He who dwells in the shelter of **the Most High** will rest in the shadow of **the Almighty**. Psalm 91:1 (NIV)

HE WHO HAS EARS LET HIM HEAR:
We all get weary, but **God** will not put more on you than you can bear. When you're in a storm, seek **God** first and rest in the shadow of **the Almighty**. **God** has charged Angels to watch over you. Turn your pressure into praise. Get a song in your spirit and sing unto the **Lord**. Everyday is significant. Yesterday's trial may provide strength for today's wilderness experience. Let your light shine by doing unto others as you would have them do unto you. Keep your countenance at all times; the look on your face is your storyboard. Pray without ceasing and teach your children to pray.

Chapter 3

'MEMBA WHEN?

But, **the Comforter**, which is **the Holy Ghost**, whom **the Father** will send in my name, he shall teach you all things, and bring all things to your remembrance, whatsoever I have said unto you. John 14:26 (KJV)

Our house was the Kool-aid house; something was always going on at our place. We grew up with common terms like 'memba instead of remember, whoopin' instead of whipping, gonna' instead of going to and 'em, 'nem and 'dem were frequently used. Don't act like you don't 'memba. If you're not ashamed of your childhood or if you know someone who grew up on the other side of the tracks, stroll with me "back down memory lane."

'Memba when almost every home had roaches? If you didn't have 'em, your cousin Pookie and Aunt Tee Tee had 'em. Oh, how soon we forget. 'Memba when we wore the same school clothes two days in a row? We had school clothes and play clothes. As soon as we came home from school, Mama used to say, "Take your school clothes off and hang 'em up."

15

When we got home, our first priority wasn't taking off clothes; we went straight to the kitchen for a snack. Sometimes we ate syrup, man'naise or ketchup "wish" sandwiches; we wished for meat between the bread. I grew up with ten siblings, but we never missed a single meal. 'Memba that free gov'ment cheese, it made the best macaroni and cheese, didn't it? Krispy Kreme didn't have anything on us, either. We poked holes in the center of Pillsbury doughboy biscuits, fried 'em in the grease on top of the stove, coated 'em in powdered sugar and when they were done we had homemade donuts.

'Memba when Mama and Daddy spent money wisely? As children, we valued money and knew it didn't grow on trees. If it did, someone cut our trees down before we moved in. On our birthdays or special occasions, we received a special treat - Daddy took us to our favorite restaurant, McDonalds or Burger King.

The entire outdoors was our playground. Mama used to say, "Ya'll go outside; kids don't need to be in grown folks business." Some days I'd go outside and run for fun. I ran fast and was too young and dumb to think Mama couldn't run fast, too. I always teased her about how much faster I could outrun her. Almost everyday, I dared her to race me. She always replied, "not now." I assumed she was afraid I would win, until one day she called my bluff. Her words "not now" didn't mean never. I was so excited; finally, I could show off my skills. I drew a starting line with chalk on the street and we stood behind it. I said, "Ready, set, go" and we took off. You don't need to know what happened next. At first, Mama let me think I would win, then zoomed pass me and stole my thunder. I fell and started crying. She must have knocked the wind out of me. Mama came to my rescue and tended to my wound. There is nothing better than a mother's love, not once did she mention the race. Rest assured my fast be'hine learned a valuable lesson. "You don't always have to win, what's important is how you play the game and how you treat the loser." Every time I look at the visible scar on my right knee, it reminds me of the race.

Speaking of visibility, 'memba those car tire swings we used to play on? Day after day, we laughed and twirled 'round and 'round until we were dizzy. We always found something to do and had so much fun outdoors. Often times, my baby brother and I climbed trees. When we lived on Mussey in Elyria, we walked the tracks and snuck in neighbor's yards to climb their fruit trees. We threw rocks and challenged each other to see who could throw the farthest. Sometimes we used the bigger rocks as a base to prop our homemade seesaws.

'Memba, dodge ball and kickball, along with red light, green light, yellow light, stop? We played Mother may I, hide and go seek, marbles, jacks and hand games. 'Memba the string hand games (i.e. Jacob's ladder, a cup-n-saucer, and the broomstick)? We were so excited to play patta cake, patta cake baker's man; make me a cake as fast as you can and Rockin' Robin tweeta leeta lee, tweeta leeta lee, tweeta leeta lee, tweeta leeta lee, tweet baby, tweet baby, tweet tweet. Don't forget hula-hoop, hopscotch and double-dutch. We used to catch butterflies and lightning bugs. We sang, "Oh lightning bugs please fly in my hand." After we caught the lightning bugs, we put 'em in a jar and poked holes in the lids.

Another favorite was Oh, Mary Mack, Mack, Mack all dressed in black, black, black, with silver buttons, buttons, buttons, all down her back, back, back. We smiled and strutted to the melody of "This away the Willoughby, Willoughby, Willoughby, and this away the Willoughby all night long." 'Memba Catalina, Matalina, whoona, sonna, wonna, tonna, okey, tokey, mokey, what's her name, what's her name? She had two eyes sticking out of her head, one was alive and one was dead. Don't ask me where we got that from, all I 'memba is we said it all the time. A man used to walk around our neighborhood saying, "Poke Chop, Smoke Chop sweet off **the Lamb***, white potatoes, stew beef, eggs and ham."*

'Memba the rioting in the early 1970's that spurred from the 1965 California Watts Riots? I 'memba it quite well 'cause it sparked riots

in our local community. After they started, Mama gathered all the kids together and specifically said, "Don't go outside." She went to work; my "bad cousins" (a term we used for acting bad, not for behaving bad) came by and persuaded my baby brother and me to pick berries. When Mama came home, my tattletale older brother met her at the door and snitched on us. Mama sent my cousins home and "whooped our tails." I tried to explain why we needed to pick food to feed the family, but Mama wasn't trying to hear it.

Speaking of food, I 'memba the first day we attended Hamilton Elementary School when Mama said she'd bring me lunch. All morning I waited and waited, but never received it. At lunchtime, I had to eat the free school lunch. 'Memba I said there were ten of us, we always ate the free lunch. Having lunch delivered by Mama was a big deal. When I went home, my siblings bragged about their lunch. I asked Mama, "What happened to my lunch?" She replied, "I dropped 'em all off at the principal's office." I never got mine. Sometimes I daydreamed in school about what that lunch must have tasted like. Isn't it funny how you remember the strangest things?

I 'memba a common phrase a teacher used, "Helen, you need to work up to your potential." They set the bar high and every time I reached it, they moved it higher. I suppose I was too comfortable with my A's and B's. My favorite teacher, Mrs Allen reminded me of Phylicia Rashad from "The Cosby Show." She was a sophisticated Nubian princess and a loveable mother figure in the classroom who taught with elegance and grace. Sometimes after school, Cuz and I stopped by her house for a visit. The girls in the class desired to grow up to be just like her. We thought she was too beautiful to be a $\mathcal{T}eacher$.

In retrospect, I learned a valuable lesson about not working up to my potential. Failure of application is a terrible thing. As a child, I was too naïve to appreciate my teacher's words of encouragement. When someone says you need to work up to your potential, work harder and apply yourself. Run toward your potential, not away from it.

I played the flute in elementary school and occasionally played for my younger siblings. One day the saddest thing happened. I came from school and searched high and low for my flute. I couldn't find it anywhere. Driscoll's Music Store had taken it back. I was devastated because it felt like they had stolen it from me. I asked Mama why she allowed them to take it and she said she could no longer make payments on it. I understood and appreciated the value of a dollar at a very early age and got over it quickly.

I didn't appreciate Driscoll's taking my flute, but I never lost my love for music. 'Memba ole school parties in Elyria? Those ole school parties more than likely brought you to the south side of town. The south side was the place to be. The Neighborhood Center, Marcell Hall, South Park, downtown and the infamous Showcase Lounge were all on the south side. The Neighborhood Center was where the teenagers danced and danced and danced. Every Friday and most Saturday nights it was jammed packed up in there. We raised the roof to Tom Browne's "Jamaica Funk", Curtis Blow's "The Breaks", and Parliament's "Flashlight." The cover charge was a dollar, sometimes two. Everybody that was somebody went to the Neighborhood Center. We had a funky good time and if a fight broke out, we fought with our fists, not with knives or guns. Y'all whippersnappers don't know nothing 'bout that.

Growing up in a family of ten was always interesting. We didn't have everything we wanted, but God provided everything we needed. Today, we refer to the past in expectation of applying meaning to our present and future.

HE WHO HAS EARS LET HIM HEAR:
Our past shapes and molds our character. Build off the foundation of the past and consider it a stepping stone, not a stumbling block.

God gave us our present day as a gift, rejoice and be glad in it. The blood of Jesus can heal your past. Run the race and persevere. Work toward your potential and press victoriously toward your mark. Remember to teach your seed about the value of a dollar. The love of money is the root of evil. Worship God, not money. Praise God we are not what we used to be.

Chapter 4

FAITH IN GOD

SECOND DAY IN THE FIRE: Friday, February 9, 2007

SCRIPTURE FOR THE DAY: He replied, "Because you have so little faith. I tell you the truth, if you have faith as small as a mustard seed, you can say to this mountain, 'Move from here to there' and it will move. Nothing will be impossible for you." Matthew 17:20-21 (NIV)

I experienced another day of unrelenting pain, exhausted and unable to sleep. I was determined to push past my body's unwillingness to function. My faith in God kept me balanced and mentally alert. The slightest thought of food made my stomach churn. I stayed in bed most of the day and reflected over my life. The Lord looked upon my affliction and pain; I could feel His mighty hand of protection as He sheltered me from the storm.

God introduced me to one of His Angels at a very young age. She sheltered me from the storms of life. My elderly Angel lived next door to Mount Nebo Church. Her house of intrigue appeared huge with a large front window and high porch. One day as I walked near her house she signaled for me to come to her. As a child, whenever people acted strange, we automatically said they were crazy. Naturally, I thought someone let the coo-coo out of her clock and I ran home as fast as I could. I wanted to tell someone, but kept her a secret instead. I needed to talk with **God** about her because my mother used to tell me that **God** hears our prayers.

I prayed for **God** to reveal what she wanted with me. Mommy's seed of servanthood grew inside of me. After a few days, my mind was at peace and I decided to go see what the woman desired of me. I walked slowly and kicked rocks until I got close to her house. As I stood across the street, she noticed me through her large window and again signaled for me. I hesitated, and then walked by faith and not by sight. Besides, if push came to shove I knew I could out-run her.

I crossed the street and kept my eyes planted on her as she opened the screen door. I trembled with fear and curiosity. When I saw her infirmities, my heart opened wide for her to come inside. She dragged her feet and both hands shook profusely. Her voice stammered and I barely understood a word she spoke. I raised my hands in the air, and then shook my head back and forth to indicate I didn't understand her. With determination, she reached into her pocket, withdrew a piece of paper and handed it to me. It contained a scribbled list of food items and I squinted to decipher the words. I read each item aloud for further clarification. She smiled; I smiled back and nodded my head "yes" several times.

She reached back into her pocket to give me a couple of dollars. I skipped to Frank's Market and hurried back to deliver her groceries. When she saw me, a peaceful countenance came on her face. I took the groceries inside, placed them on the table, returned her change and smiled as she handed me back fifty cents. Instantly, I fell in love with her. I thanked **God** for placing her in my life. I wanted to hug her, but I didn't, at least not that time.

*After that instance, I hugged her every time I saw her. Almost everyday, I stopped by to see if she needed anything. We became confidants and sometimes we "talked story." The more we talked, the more I understood her. Her countenance changed whenever I stopped by. My desire was to serve her as she covered me with love and sheltered me from the storm. My heart literally broke when she passed away. My Angel taught me to trust in the **Lord**, to walk by faith and not by sight. This was the Angel that taught me to physically shake (as to remove/ward off) anything that was not of **God**. I never knew her name, but I remember her sweet voice.*

My older sister called and when I answered, she didn't recognize my voice. She replied, "Who is this?" I said, "Helen, I'm sick and I lost my voice." She sounded heavy-burdened and replied, "I really need to talk to you, my Sistah!" Then, someone knocked at her door and she said she'd call me back later tonight. I couldn't get my mind off my sister. I got out of bed several times to tidy the house, but to no avail. The unending sickness lingered over me like a shadow of darkness, my soul was weary and I needed to rest. I went back to bed and lay down.

When my husband came home from work I was still in bed, and he asked if I needed anything. I asked for medicine. He dispensed it, placed his hand on my forehead, and prayed. I couldn't hear or understand a word he prayed, but Mama's voice echoed in my mind, "Your husband is your silent strength." His whispered prayer renewed my strength and calmed the storm. I was at peace and kept still. A few minutes later, I got out of bed and tended to the affairs of my household. My body was weak, but my faith was strong. Eventually, I made my way back to bed.

I tossed and turned in bed, but found little to no comfort. I couldn't sleep and my sister's words echoed in my mind, "I really need to talk to you, my Sistah." I hummed Quincy Jones' lyrics from The Color Purple, "Sister, you've been on my mind." I coughed, spat, coughed and spat. I needed to rid myself of the results from the coughs. I got up, went to the kitchen for a plastic cup, returned to my bedroom and placed the cup on my nightstand. Every time I coughed, I spat in the cup. The cup became my spit container.

Speaking of spit container's, my maternal grandfather, Papa chewed tobacco and forever spat into his metal "spit can." When he coughed, it sounded like he coughed up his insides and then spat it into his can. He always rocked back and forth in his rocking chair in front of the coal stove in the family room. His spit can was sedentary on the floor beside him. He had a retractable cane in one hand and a pipe in the other. He loved to scare children and I tried to stay out of his reach.

During one visit, I reminded Mama how scared I was of Papa and begged her to sleep downstairs. Usually, whenever we visited Papa and Mommy we would spend the night and sleep in the upstairs' bedrooms. The only way upstairs was through a guest room, the off-limits living area and lastly through Papa's bedroom. Mama used to say, "Don't pay Papa no 'tention when he tries to scare you". She knew that wasn't an option; he knew how to get your attention!

While in bed, he pretended to be asleep. I could never discern if he was awake or asleep because of how he covered himself completely from head-to-toe. For several minutes, I would watch his every move as he lay completely still; I was convinced he was asleep. I mustered up every ounce of faith in me. I was only three years old; my faith was probably the size of a mustard seed. Anyway, I tiptoed into his bedroom. Halfway between the door and stairwell he outstretched his arm from beneath the cover, grabbed hold of me and loudly bellowed, "Meow-w-w." I cried a river and trembled with fear as he laughed repeatedly until he decided to let me go. I didn't sleep well that night and the next morning I stayed upstairs until he was out of bed.

Papa had an entrepreneurial spirit: he bought land, cut down trees and constructed four houses. He named his subdivision in Elyria on

South 2nd Street, Noel's Ville. His family lived in one and he rented the other three. He earned respect and his good reputation preceded him in the neighborhood and city. Papa died on February 7, 1968. **Lord** knows how much I miss him. I desire to hear him say, "Meowww." His legacy to me was "Fear Not."

I lay in bed wide-awake and chuckled as I thought of Papa's signature "Meow's!" I found strength in my childhood memories. Papa taught me to exercise my faith, not to fear the unknown and to cover myself (literally) from head-to-toe. My throat was raw and I coughed, spat, coughed and spat in my makeshift "spit can." I couldn't sleep, so I got up and read my Bible.

HE WHO HAS EARS LET HIM HEAR:
We are never alone. During sickness and disease, **God** will soothe your soul. Everyone goes through the furnace of afflictions. **God** does not take pleasure in our suffering. When your heart is troubled, keep the faith. Find comfort in the Bible. Trust and believe in **the Word** of God and lean not on your own understanding. The grace of God is sufficient in the fire. **Jesus** died on the cross and His blood covers us. He suffered for our transgressions. Exercise your faith and fear not.

Chapter 5

THE HARVEST

A man reaps what he sows. The one who sows to please his sinful nature, from that nature will reap destruction; the one who sows to please **the Spirit**, from **the Spirit** will reap eternal life. Let us not become weary in doing good, for at the proper time we will reap a harvest if we do not give up. Therefore, as we have opportunity, let us do good to all people, especially to those who belong to the family of believers. Galatians 6:7-10 (NIV)

When we moved from Lorain to Elyria, I grew close to our elderly landlords, Ma and Pa. My parents taught us to respect our elders. They instilled in us proper terms of address and explained why we extended them common courtesies. Under no circumstance, did we address adults or authority figures by their first name. When children walked past an adult, they spoke first. Today, many have failed to train up children in **the Way** they should go. As a result, they lack self-respect and disrespect authority figures. **God** commands us to honor and obey our parents with a promise that we may enjoy long life on earth. We didn't have a choice whether or not to honor and obey our parents. Maybe that is why Baby Boomers are living longer and enjoying life. Baby Boomers had it good, quite possibly because we felt the hand of **God** upon us. *I 'memba an* **Omnipresent** *picture of* **Jesus**, *called "The Invitation" hanging* *in almost every home you entered. In the picture, **Jesus'** hands are outstretched to us. The picture still speaks to my spirit.*

I can picture Pa; he was a tall elderly man with gray hair. He took a special interest in me and would promise to buy me some "pretty little girl clothes" at Elyria City. He extended his hand to me and taught me how to garden at the tender age of "7." We took advantage of the fertile ground in our backyard; it was the perfect place to create beauty. During autumn and winter, I learned patience; springtime was my season. Every spring, Pa and I planted our garden. He tilled the soil and instructed me to remove the big rocks. As a child, I spoke like a child and questioned why? He replied, "Seeds should be planted on good soil, not shallow ground. Rocks hinder plants from receiving moisture." I asked what shallow meant and he said, "Shallow means not deep and seeds need to be rooted in deep ground in order to grow." I smiled, removed the big rocks from the soil, and placed them in the bucket. We made near perfect rows and individual holes for each plant and/or seed. We planted cabbage, greens, corn, peppers, tomatoes, onions, beans, and cucumbers. Lastly, we covered the holes with a rake. When my load was too much to bear, I emptied it on the railroad tracks next to our house. We lived within fifty feet of the tracks. The trains ran nightly like clockwork, but we managed to sleep in spite of the noise. Almost every time we gardened, Pa reminded me of his promise.

*After sowing seeds, my job was watering and removing weeds that sprouted up next to the harvest. Everyday, I anxiously waited for the plants and seeds to spring forth into a marvelous harvest. Mommy rejoiced in the harvest, too. She canned fruits and vegetables religiously in glass mason jars and stored them on the shelves. The green beans, tomatoes, jellies, apples, peaches, pears, blackberries and chow-chow (relish) were her precious preservatives. On cloudy days, I faithfully watered our garden and on rainy days, I looked out the window as **the Gardener** watered it. Sometimes after the rain, my baby brother and I went outdoors to catch night crawlers. My uncles fished, but didn't* like to catch worms. *My baby brother and I often bet one another to see who could catch the most worms. Usually, I caught the most because my long fingers gripped the worms better than his. Those poor worms didn't stand a chance; we stored them in plastic containers with dirt and sold them to our uncles the next day.*

Speaking of crawlers, one day I went next door to visit Pa. He sat upright in his living room chair with his legs wide open and a pierced look in his eye. Like a serpent in the garden, Pa hissed harsh words to me, words he never should have spoken to a little girl. They weren't shallow words because they deeply permeated my root. He quickly reminded me of his promise to buy me some "pretty little girl clothes." I realized his motives were never pure. I left and buried my love for gardening in my heart. The devil wanted my load to be too heavy to bear, to keep me off track and to stop me from planting seeds. The devil is a liar. I continued to plant seeds, but not in Pa's backyard.

The seeds I planted as a child (The Fruits of My Labor) taught me how to be fruitful and multiply. As an adult, I understand why you reap what you sow. Following are a few testimonies from seeds sown:

"My 'sistah' from another mother. You have always been able to pierce my soul. You are one of two women whom I most admire. I admire your strength, determination, and steadfastness. Don't play with this sister. You are phenomenal and have been instrumental to me during my 'time in the fire.' Your words are always kind but firm, exact but reaffirming, uplifting and never condemning. You have a personality that can turn vinegar into a sweet Italian Moscato wine. You are the Angel God sent me and I love you. "

Bridget

"As gold is purified through the fire, so has our friendship and sisterhood been purified. You're a precious gem who adds value to everyone you encounter, to include me. Many seeds were planted in my life. Over the years, your fellowship and spirit have watered my seeds and have enabled this bud to bloom into a beautiful rose. God used you to help me grow despite the thorns in my life. Thank you for helping me through many fires. To whom much is given, much is required. God knew my life required a sister, a friend and a mentor such as you. Go and speak to the multitudes, God has prepared you for such a time as this."

Trae

"I believe God sends Angels to protect and guide those He loves on earth. I met my God-sent Angel around September 2003 while stationed in Hawaii – my paradise on earth. Helen came into my life when God saw my need for a friend and confidant. She listened and consoled without judging or criticizing. We laughed and cried, sang, and danced. We prayed. I rode on her wings of strength and wisdom and became stronger and wiser. We are each other's keeper, I thank God for the woman I have become and thank Him for sending Helen. She is my Angel."

Myrna

"My beautiful sister Helen, from the beginning I could see your heart, obviously not as closely as Father God, but truly your heart shines for all to see. Because your heart is so overflowing with the love of God, it is priceless to all the lives you touch. Even though some may not know nor understand the magnitude of God's love and touch through your spirit of giving, I've always known. This book is a testament of how the hand of God has always been over your life. Because you are truly a woman after God's own heart, I have always said to you 'You are like David, one of God's beloved.' I love you. May God continue to bless you. May He bless and prosper this book to touch the lives of those who READ it and bless those that HEAR about it to step out and be a DOER of the Word of God."

Blessings Always, Twaina

"Helen, it's hard to put into words how knowing you has influenced my life. I've been friends with you longer than any other friend except one friend in my hometown. We've been hanging in there for thirteen years. I love you, because you are genuine and true. I love you because you are consistent and loving. I love you because you are selfless and strong. You're the best example of a mother, daughter, sister and friend than anyone I know. What you have given me is a true commitment to friendship. To hang in there even when it's hard. I've learned the value of having a sister that isn't born of the same mother. I love you the same as either of my sisters. I'm closer to you than I Am my biological sisters or mother. You are truly a gift to me. You are the real deal, and you really have a heart for women and friendships. I love you and I'm thankful that you are in my life."

Audrey

You reap what you sow. When you plant seed with right motives, it will multiply and produce a beautiful harvest. In the Bible, Jesus says in The Parable of the Weeds:

"The kingdom of heaven is like a man who sowed good seed in his field. But while everyone was sleeping, his enemy came and sowed weeds among the wheat and went away. When the wheat sprouted and formed heads, then the weeds also appeared. The owner's servants came to him and said, 'Sir, didn't you sow good seed in your field? Where then did the weeds come from?' 'An enemy did this,' he replied. "The servants asked him, 'Do you want us to go and pull them up?' 'No,' he answered, 'because while you are pulling the weeds, you may root up the wheat with them. Let both grow together until the harvest. At that time I will tell the harvesters: First collect the weeds and tie them in bundles to be burned; then gather the wheat and bring it into my barn.'"

Matthew 13:24-30 (NIV)

The Parable of the Weeds Explained:

"Then he left the crowd and went into the house. His disciples came to him and said, "Explain to us the parable of the weeds in the field." He answered, "The one who sowed the good seed is **the Son of Man**. The field is the world, and the good seed stands for the sons of the kingdom. The weeds are the sons of the evil one, and the enemy who sows them is the devil. The harvest is the end of the age, and the harvesters are angels. As the weeds are pulled up and burned in the fire, so it will be at the end of the age. The **Son of Man** will send out his angels, and they will weed out of his kingdom everything that causes sin and all who do evil. They will throw them into the fiery furnace, where there will be weeping and gnashing of teeth. Then the righteous will shine like the sun in the kingdom of their **Father**. He who has ears, let him hear. "

Matthew 13:36-43 (NIV)

Our front yard extended to the fields across the street where there was an abundance of fruit. My baby brother and I loved to pick blackberries and strawberries. The strawberries were the first fruits to ripen in the spring and we anticipated their splendor. One day, in the midst of our excitement, we wandered far off and lost track of time. We hardly lost our sense of direction; the light of God directed our path and we didn't fear the unknown. Unexpectedly, we came upon the most beautiful harvest where strawberry beds and blackberry vines were plentiful. The slender blackberry branches adorned the vineyard. The ripe fruit fell off the vine by the touch of our hands. We couldn't believe our eyes as we licked our lips and sampled the harvest. We picked as many berries as we could, our containers runneth over.

We hurried home with the overflow to share "The Good News" and couldn't wait to take some to Mommy; she said they were the most beautiful berries she had ever seen and made us blackberry dumplings. The next day we went into the fields in search of the harvest, but couldn't find it. We never found it again, but rejoiced in what God had shown us. Lord knows we searched often. Sometimes, we trampled over snakes and whoever saw it first screamed, "Snaaaaaaaaake", we ran zigzag as fast as we could until we were out of the fields. We stayed out of the fields the day we saw the snake, but returned the next (we wept for a night, but joy came in the morning).

When we were bored, we created our own joy. One day, I taught my baby brother how to ride a bicycle. I never understood why he was so afraid. Several times, he ran straight into the wall. For some reason, every time he turned to the right or left he lifted up his hands off the handlebars. I told him repeatedly to just hold on and everything would be all right. I was so proud when he finally held on and soared on his own wings.

At an early age, I became my younger siblings' keeper and took them under my wing. I felt responsible for them and longed to shelter them from the storms of life. In 1991, my baby brother was diagnosed with Multiple Sclerosis. Over the years, he has gotten progressively worse and currently he resides in a nursing home. "My brother, this earthly body is temporal, you hold on because everything's gonna' be all right. Remember our favorite phrase, 'Long live **the King**!'"

When we lived on Mussey Avenue, the trestle (framework used to carry a railroad across a depression) was about a ten-minute walk down the railroad tracks. One day, my older sister, younger brother and I decided to fish down by the river. We found three juice cartons, a few long sticks, some string and a couple slices of bread. Next, we poked holes in the cartons and tied string around the sticks. Back then, neighborhoods were safe and kids had freedom to roam. We walked down the railroad tracks with our homemade rods in hand. Shortly afterwards we reached the trestle, walked down the valley and then canvassed the area for a safe place to cast our nets.

We came upon a rock that looked safe and stood on it, prepped our rods and used the bread for bait. None of us understood the danger of mud and seaweed on **the Rock**. We were all under the age of ten and didn't have any business at the river. If Mama had known, three *whoopins would have had our names on them. We were so excited when we saw the minnows in the water. Like fishermen, my brother cast his rod to the left, my sister watched over us as* **the Mediator** *and I cast mine to the right. Within seconds, my feet started to wander off* **the Rock** *in the direction of the water. Instantly with the strongest force, my sister outstretched her arm and snatched me to dry ground. My brother and I thought my sister had supernatural powers and stood dazed with our mouths and eyes wide open. We left* **the Rock** *and agreed we wouldn't tell anyone. Whenever my sister desired special treatment or favor, she casually reminded me of when she saved my life. Unbelievably, none of us could swim.* **God** *didn't plan for me to walk through the valley of the shadow of death at the river.* **Jesus** *is* **the Rock** *of our salvation.*

HE WHO HAS EARS LET HIM HEAR:

Respect elders. Train up children in the fear and admonition of the **Lord**. The harvest belongs to **Christ**, the firstfruit. There is an appropriate time and season for everything under the sun. **God** determines when we sow and when we reap. In between seasons, He prunes us in the form of trials and tribulations. The pruning stage shapes and molds our character; sometimes this stage is painful. Satan's weeds will tempt you because he desires to steal, kill, and destroy your seed. Temptations come in many forms, to include threats and promises. When the seed is nourished, it gives life and energy to **the Root**. The harvest speaks of healing and restoration, deliverance, completion and maturation. The harvest is worth the wait. **God** has given us the authority to trample over snakes and to overcome the power of the enemy. Don't be afraid to cast your net into the river. When storms come, continue to stand on "**the Rock**." His outstretched hand will deliver you from the hand of the enemy and make you "fishers of men." There is no condemnation for whatever secrets you have.

Chapter 6

THE CHILDREN OF GOD

THIRD DAY IN THE FIRE: Saturday, February 10, 2007

SCRIPTURE FOR THE DAY: But you are a chosen people, a royal priesthood, a Holy nation, a people belonging to God, that you may declare the praises of Him who called you out of darkness into his Wonderful light. 1 Peter 2:9 (NIV)

I rose to yet another day of unbearable pain and agony, physically exhausted with every inch of my body experiencing some degree of pain. The head throbs, continuous back spasms and aches in joints I never knew existed were ailments associated with my weak stomach. I questioned where to turn for comfort? In my distress, I called on the name of the Lord, tuned the television to The Spirit channel and found comfort as I listened to the sweet sound of gospel music. I was too sick to attend my firstborn son's end of season basketball celebration, so I encouraged my family to attend without me. My body was too weak to get out of bed, the sickness had manifested. I still had the strongest desire to reach my sister. I called her several times, but to no avail.

Late afternoon, I felt like my test was over and I desired a moment just for me. Mother Helen's seed of excellence ignited inside of me and I yearned for a beauty makeover. Occasionally, I treat myself like Queen Sheba and this day I sought restoration. My trial deserved the red carpet treatment; I longed for a manicure and pedicure.

I 'memba our wall-to-wall carpet installation on West Avenue. We thought we had died and went straight to heaven. We were "movin' on up" like George Jefferson. "Y'all don't hear me!" The carpet installation was a significant milestone for our family. Mama had it installed mostly downstairs, but the **Carpenter** *laid a foundation on the stairwell, too. I was in need of a secret place and often sat alone on the carpeted stairwell to meditate. When my friends came by I said, "Please take your shoes off before you walk on our new carpet." I continually rubbed my hands back and forth over the surface. It was so soft and felt so good under my feet.*

As for Queen Sheba, I 'memba when my older sister got mad at something I said and threw a case knife at me, it just barely missed my head. Did she intend to harm me - did she hate me that much? We went through our high school years and didn't speak to one another. I passed her in school one day and she treated me like a complete stranger. It bothered me; but I pretended I was fine. We didn't resolve our differences until I was much older and in the military. Once I came home from the military and asked Mama to prepare a few of my favorite foods, homemade biscuits, and peach cobbler. We have not, because we ask not. Mama woke up early the next morning and prepared a gourmet breakfast with homemade biscuits. I lay in bed as the sweet aroma of breakfast filled the air. My older sister stopped by the house and yelled through the door, "Queen Sheba, yo' Mama fixed you breakfast, it's time to get up and eat." I got up; we laughed about her comment and ate the breakfast Mama prepared.

As time passed, we grew closer and God softened her heart. She opened up one day and explained her hatred for me. She said she hated me because I was always Mama's favorite. The favor was not from my Mama, but my Father in Heaven favored me. His favor didn't seem fair. God said to forgive and forget, and I obeyed His word. Today my sister who once hated me is one of my favorite. I Am my sister's keeper.

Mama worked hard to make ends meet and she didn't have much time to spend with any of her children, but I made her spend time with me. She and Daddy separated when I was six. Mama made ends meet with what she had. She normally came home from work tired, ate dinner and laid on the couch to rest. Whenever she lay on the couch, I sat at her feet. If she sat on it, so did I, right beside her, practically on top of her. Mama used to say, "I can't even fart without you right beside me to smell it" and other times she would let it rip and fart right on me. I suppose I deserved it. I knew she was tired, but as much as she needed to rest, I needed to be beside her.

In keeping with my spirit of excellence, I showered, dressed and drove to the nail salon. Upon entering, the attendant said, "Hello, what can I do for you today?" I replied, "The works, a manicure, pedicure and eyebrow waxing." He told me to pick a color and directed me towards the pedicure section. I submitted, walked to the chair, propped in it, took my shoes off, turned on the back massage, smiled at the attendant and said, "Please make my water hot." Did I mention how much I love to have my feet washed?

After I got my beauty treatment, I went next door to the grocery store. My primary purchase was collard greens. My husband bought one bag at the grocery store the day before, but one bag wasn't enough. While in the store, I called my sister again, but didn't get an answer. Her words from the day before consumed me and I couldn't stop thinking about her. I telephoned Mama and asked if she knew what my sister needed to talk to me about. She replied, "No, but she called me to ensure she had your correct number." I paid for the groceries and headed home.

I arrived home, washed my hands and boiled the smoked turkey. I put the greens in the kitchen sink and therapeutically labored over them. I added the greens to the turkey, seasoned them with a little bit of this and a little bit of that and poured in olive oil from the jar beneath the stove. I hesitated to sample them because my stomach was too weak to digest food. Since greens are my favorite, I felt compelled to taste them to see if they were good. All I could taste was oil (grease).

Almost every household had grease cans on top of the stoves and red strings of peppers hanging in kitchens. One morning when we lived on Mussey Avenue, my older sister and I ran downstairs for breakfast. The Cornflakes was out of reach in the cupboard above the stove and we contemplated a resolution. She opened the oven door and said, "Stand on it and pass me the cereal." I didn't think twice about it, she was my keeper. I raised one foot at a time and balanced myself onto the door. When I raised my arms, I lost my balance. The stove tilted slightly away from the wall, it almost tipped over and the grease can fell on the floor. Grease spilled everywhere. We slipped and slid all over, the soles of our feet were covered in grease. My older brother overheard the commotion, ran into the kitchen and yelled, "Ew-ew, I'm a tell Mama and y'all gonna get a whoopin." Mama was at work. We mopped the floor and tried our best to return the floor to its original condition. In school, all I thought about was spilled grease and my whoopin'.

Mama had a whoopin' with my name on it because my older brother couldn't hold water. My sister and I intentionally walked home slowly, kicking every rock in sight. When we got home, Mama asked, "Which of you want a whoopin' first?" "Me," my sister replied. My younger siblings slid around on the kitchen floor as if it was a homemade slip-n-slide. I ran upstairs to put on some extra clothes; I had the whole day to come up with a plan to soften the blow. You never knew which weapon Mama would use against you. She used tree switches, extension cords, belts or the orange Hotwheel's racetrack to whoop us. My older brother always lurked in the shadow of a whoopin'. If we picked flimsy switches, he transformed into Daniel Boone and practically cut the tree down for Mama to whoop us.

Consequently, after the first whoopin' Mama was practically out of breath. In desperation, we spat on our hands and rubbed it on our face to make it appear we cried up a storm. When it was my turn, I thought no weapon could prosper. Donning two pairs of pants, I wondered if my tattletale brother would detect my secret. Mama was tired and all I needed was an ample supply of spit. Mama used to say, "Whoopin' you is gonna hurt me more than it's gonna hurt you." I had the perfect solution--don't whoop me then. Now that I'm a mother, I feel your pain Mama. I felt it back then, too. Whoopin' ain't easy, but sometimes you have to take matters into your own hands.

That evening as we retired to bed, my husband tossed and turned as I coughed, spat, coughed and spat throughout the night. Neither of us could sleep. I got up and read my Bible.

HE WHO HAS EARS LET HIM HEAR:

My Papa died February "7", 1968 (my wilderness experience began almost forty years later on the night of February "7", 2007). Almost forty years ago, the late Dr. Martin Luther King said he saw the Promised Land in his last speech, "I see the Promised Land." The children of God have been in the wilderness for forty years, but 2007 is a year of completion. Get ready to cross over to new beginnings in 2008. His children are the chosen generation. God tells us if we are faithful over a few things that He will make us rulers over many. Children also need discipline and correction. Spare the rod and spoil the child. We are a royal priesthood. Forgive those who have hurt you. Seek God and reap His favor.

Chapter "7"

TEMPTATION

When tempted, no one should say, 'God is tempting me.' For God cannot be tempted by evil, nor does he tempt anyone; but each one is tempted when, by his own evil desire, he is dragged away and enticed. Then, after desire has conceived, it gives birth to sin; and sin, when it is full-grown, gives birth to death.
James 1:13-15 (NIV)

One day, my "bad cousins" stopped by my house; we walked from the Southside of Elyria toward the downtown Police Station and "talked story." We spotted a po-go stick in front of a house and one of us dared the others to jump on it. I can't recall who jumped first, but within minutes it was monkey-see, monkey-do. After we all jumped, we dropped it and ran from the scene. Our adrenaline started to flow and we were up to "no good" from then on. On our way home, one of my cousins pointed to a plant on a porch and said, "I bet your mom would love to have that beautiful plant, she deserves it." Our thoughts shifted to "Are you thinking what I'm thinking?" We snuck on the porch and stole the plant.

I don't 'memba which of us stole the first plant, but when we got home each of us had at least one stolen plant in our hands. When we got back to my house, we looked through the curtain and saw my older sister and boyfriend in the living room reading their Bibles. We snuck the plants around the back, put them on the patio and then decided to go back to steal some more. My cousins and I stole about ten plants and a couple lawn chairs, too. We covered the patio in beautiful stolen plants. Before going to bed, I brought them indoors and decorated the dining room.

Speaking of stealing, Cuz forgive me while I tell this story. One day my favorite cousin and I rode our bicycles to the dairy on 16th Street. Cuz still had a little "Ely Village hood" in her and I dared her to steal some milk off the truck. Before I could say "sike", she was on the truck. Almost instantly, a man stepped off the truck holding Cuz by her armpits. She kicked her legs back and forth so hard that he had to let her go. Cuz ran down the hill so fast that she forgot her bike. The man started to interrogate me, but I stuck to my answer, "I don't know her." I told him I met her earlier that day and he drilled me until we were both tired. I wasn't about to snitch on Cuz, we didn't roll like that y'all. After awhile, he went back into the dairy and there I stood alone with two bikes. I thought about leaving Cuz's bike, but my conscience got the best of me. I rolled both bikes down the hill. When I got to Cuz's house, I had scratch marks on both ankles and legs. I went upstairs and she was sitting on the floor in her room lookin' crazy. Cuz begged me not to tell anyone about the milk incident, and we laughed until we almost peed on ourselves.

The morning after we stole the plants, Mama came in my bedroom, sat at the foot of my bed and said, "Helen, where did all those plants come from?" Initially, I imitated Papa and pretended to be asleep. She asked me again and I jokingly replied, "We took 'em off some porches for you because you deserve 'em." After I answered, I felt so ashamed. She shook her head in disgust and left the room. My heart sank to the floor; the shame on Mama's face hurt me. I felt like I hurt my best friend.

I attempted to go back to sleep, but my guilty conscience kept me awake. A few minutes later, I got out of bed and went downstairs. Mama was sedentary in the corner chair and when I glanced at her she ignored me. I walked slowly into the dining room, it looked like a greenhouse and the stolen plants choked me. I needed someone to remove the thorns. Mama gave me the silent treatment most of the day.

Later that day, my "bad cousins" came by. Mama made them go home and put me under punishment. Later that evening, Mama came to me and said, "In all my years, I would have never thought you would do something like this. Do you realize you could've been killed?" She elaborated on plants and their symbolic meaning, reaping and sowing, and how much time it must have taken to grow such beautiful plants. Then she reminded me that some people save plants from funerals, in memory of their loved ones. I could no longer contain myself; I broke down and cried a river. I tried to rationalize why we stole them and reminded her that she deserved them. She unselfishly said, "I don't deserve stolen plants from someone else's labor." Her last words penetrated like a knife when she said, "I expected that behavior from others, but not from you." Our parent's expectations were one thing; living up to them was another story.

Speaking of "bad cousins" (one of which happened to be my favorite cousin), we were inseparable; sometimes we dressed alike, too. I 'memba the day her family moved from Ely Village to a beautiful home on 13th Street. Cuz and I were finally able to attend the same school. My favorite cousin came to school like a bully beatin' up most of my closest friends. She was out of control. At recess, I witnessed Cuz beatin' up my tallest girlfriend, she had the nerve to jump up and punch her in the face. My friends began to disassociate themselves from me because my cousin was a bully. Without a doubt, I had to do something. I thought long and hard about the exact words to say to make her stop. I told Cuz, "If you don't stop beatin' up all my friends, I'm gonna' stop being your cousin."

At that time, I didn't know I couldn't stop being her cousin. Cuz and I fit together like a hand in a glove and my words pierced her like a knife. One day, Cuz got beat up by one of my friends. I asked her why she got beat up and Cuz said, "I didn't fight her back because I didn't want you to stop being my cousin."

Mama's words spoke life into me and my words spoke life into my cousin. I lived with the shame of stealing season after season and vowed never to disappoint Mama like that again for as long as I lived. Prayerfully, I have kept my promise.

HE WHO HAS EARS LET HIM HEAR:
God has granted all of us a certain amount of grace, mercy, and peace but certain acts rob us of our inheritance. The devil comes like a thief in the night to steal our joy and he'll use anything or anyone to tempt us, even family members. The devil tempted Jesus; rest assured he also tempts us, just as Christ overcame temptation, so can we. Everything the devil means for bad, God can use it for good. God knows our hearts and He forgives us. There is no condemnation for those in Christ Jesus. Death and life are in the power of the tongue, but Jesus came so that we would have life and have it more abundantly. Somebody is praying for your deliverance from sin. Live according to the Fruits of the Spirit (love, joy, peace, patience, kindness, goodness, faithfulness, gentleness, and self-control) not according to the sinful nature.

Chapter 8

SET THE CAPTIVES FREE

FOURTH DAY IN THE FIRE: Sunday, February 11, 2007

SCRIPTURE FOR THE DAY: The Spirit of the Sovereign Lord is on me, because the Lord has anointed me to preach good news to the poor. He has sent me to bind up the brokenhearted, to proclaim freedom for the captives and release from darkness for the prisoners. Isaiah 61:1 (NIV)

I coughed, spat, coughed and spat like Papa in my "spit can" most of the night. Around 4:00 a.m., in between spats, I felt like I had to vomit and leaped out of bed. The teaspoon of greens I sampled a few hours earlier didn't agree with my stomach. When I vomited, it sounded like thunder shut up in my bones. My husband heard me and got a cold compress to place on my forehead. I sat on the bathroom floor for a while listless and lethargic wrestling with the pain that permeated every fiber of my being. As I suffered, my body was light as a feather. Lord, please take this cup! I vomited several more times and eventually returned to bed. I coughed, spat, coughed and spat. In the morning, my husband awoke tired;

neither one of us slept, but I encouraged him to attend church. Today was Pastor's birthday celebration.

When we were kids, we had to go to church every Sunday. Mama and Daddy separated when I was six, but we continued to be a close-knit family. Daddy came by to visit us almost everyday. If we didn't see him on Monday, rest assured we saw him on Tuesday. After they separated, Daddy continued to attend New Hope Missionary Baptist Church in Lorain and I often spent the weekend with him so I could attend, too. My dad is the senior member of his church; he's been a member since 1954. As soon as we stepped inside the church, my eyes shifted to the pianist and songstress, Ms. Nettie Mae Jackson. Whenever she would sing, heaven opened up and her voice brought tears to my eyes. God made my long fingers to play a piano and I've always desired to play and sing in church. One day, I'll play and sing in the heavenly choir. God always gave me a new song to sing.

After my family left for church, I turned the television to The Spirit channel and hummed the lyrics to a few songs; the sweet sound of gospel music soothed my soul. The pain from my illness intensified throughout the morning and the thought of food made my stomach churn. Hours later, my family returned and I was still in bed. My husband fixed a bowl of greens, I asked him how they were and he replied, "They taste good." I told him I thought they tasted oily and he reminded me of the additional oil from the smoked turkey. I contemplated if I should taste them again, but decided against it since my digestive system was so unbalanced. I went back to bed and continued listening to The Spirit channel.

I 'memba when I enjoyed music class in junior high school. The music Teacher played the piano and attempted to show me how to sing from my diaphragm. I 'member a musical concert I participated in when a girl named Kim sang, "You Light up My Life" by Debbie Boone. The lyrics and melody settled in my spirit and have been a part of me ever since. One day, the most bizarre thing happened. The music **Teacher** *cornered me in a dark room and spoke words that struck like a piano out of tune. Words he shouldn't have spoken to a teenage girl. After that, I could barely stand to be in his presence. Whenever I saw him, if he walked to the left, I purposely walked to the right. If he walked towards me, I turned around and went in the opposite direction. His job was to administer music and his words disappointed me. He tried to steal my melody and take me off key. Music was my passion; he caused me to distance myself from the class. The devil is a liar. I continued to sing, but not in his music class.*

I have a picture that inspires me, by Ken Brown, "The Touch of the Master's Hand," and it reads: "Whenever your life is out of tune and no melody soothes your soul, look to the **Master** whose gentle touch will bless you and make you whole. Like an old violin with so little worth, a life may be far less than grand, but may be transformed in a moment you see, By the Touch of the Master's Hand."

The hand of **God** has always protected me. Mommy's seed of servanthood consumed me all weekend. I called my sister several times, but could not reach her. Finally, she answered the phone and poured her heart out to me. Her confessions touched me and my heart opened wide for her to come inside. My sister sighed and said that her son, my beloved nephew, was going to jail for aggravated murder. While crying she remarked, "He'll be in jail for twenty years, I'll be sixty-three years old when he gets out. I feel like my child has literally been ripped from my womb. Sistah, I'm in the most excruciating pain and everybody says to be strong, but it's easier said than done." Like never before, I desired to take away my sister's pain. I cried out, "**Jesus, Jesus, Jesus**."

Many years ago, my sister saved my life at the river and I desperately wanted to save hers. We cried together and I searched for the right words to comfort her troubled mind. I desired to strengthen her without using **the Word** strong. My sister stated, "I need you to pray for me." My voice was weak and I needed restoration for my debilitated soul. With every ounce of strength in my feeble body, I stepped out on faith, fell down on my knees, lifted my hands to God and cast my rod to comfort her. As she cried out to the Lord, I prayed fervently. I reminded her of when she walked with **the Lord**, how much she used to read the Bible and how her prayers covered my "bad cousins" and me when we stole those plants for Mama. I replied, "The devil wants to destroy your seed, the devil is a liar and you hold on my 'sistah.' No weapon formed against you shall prosper; this is the year of completion and rest. God is ready to finish what He started in you." I said, "God will set the captives free and I love you my sister." She agreed that it was time for her to come home to **Jesus**.

Before we hung up, she said, "You need to go back to the doctor to get some 'scripts.'" I had no idea what scripts were, so I asked, "What's scripts?" She answered, "Scripts, my sistah, prescription drugs, you need some antibiotics." We laughed and I promised to go back to the doctor the next day.

Her words "I feel like a baby has literally been ripped from my womb" reminded me of when I was a senior in high school. I thought about when my favorite cousin had a baby in her womb. Cuz moved to Cleveland with her dad's side of the family in 1979 after her mother, Rosella, died. I was literally devastated by her death and even more so when Cuz moved from Elyria to Cleveland.

In May 1983, I celebrated the miraculous birth of my favorite cousin's firstborn. Her delivery date was mid-May and on May 12, I decided to pay her a visit. When I arrived at Madea's (Cuz's grandmother) house, she informed me of Cuz's admittance to the hospital a few days earlier. She said, "I thought you knew, baby." I rushed to the hospital and as fate would have it, as soon as I walked in the door, Cuz decided she had labored long enough and it was time to give birth.

She had been in hard labor for twenty two hours straight and all of a sudden--bam! All I said was "Hey-ey Girl." Cuz yelled, "Helon-n-n-n-n-n-n" and started having contractions. With my eyes wide open, in harmony I echoed "he-he-who-who" right along with Cuz, until they wheeled her into the delivery room. The doctors said I couldn't go in with her so I waited patiently outside the door for the baby to be born. I was a nervous wreck. Cuz asked if I would name the baby, I graciously accepted and named her Tiana Rose. At the time, I didn't know what her name meant, but **God** knew. Her first name is a variant of Christian and her middle name is symbolic of flower. We rejoiced in the new birth. **Jesus** is **the Life**. At the tender age of eighteen, **God** allowed me to witness a miracle.

God miraculously strengthened me after speaking with my sister. I got out of bed, ironed my children's clothes for the week, and hung them in their closets. It was much needed therapy for my soul. As a teenager, I found shelter from the storms in my upstairs bedroom as I ironed clothes, did homework, sang songs, wrote poems and read the Bible. I kept my room spic-n-span clean. When I ironed, I hung each item neatly in my closet. My life required order; my room was a place of order.

When I went to bed, I coughed and spat in my spit can until about 3:00 a.m. I couldn't sleep, so I got up and read my Bible.

HE WHO HAS EARS LET HIM HEAR:
When we fail to seek **God**, we become prisoners enslaved in the sinful nature of this world. **God** desires to set the captives free from the bondages of sin through freedom in **Christ**. As Christians, we have to experience a new birth of **the Spirit** rather than the flesh. When we allow situations and circumstances to

become strongholds in our lives we live in bondage. God will do whatever is necessary and go to great lengths to get our attention. Call on the name of Jesus when your pain seems too heavy to bear. He'll bring you through the fire. If you give up, you may stunt the growth of your seed or never give birth to the seed. Rebuke the devil and break the chains of bitterness, pride and envy. Although you are tempted or you may stray away from God, He is ever-present and His arms are always open wide to invite you into the Kingdom. Angels rejoice in homecomings. Dedicate or rededicate your life to Jesus and watch Him move mountains.

Chapter 9

THE REUNION

Bear with each other and forgive whatever grievances you may have against one another. Forgive as the **Lord** forgave you. And over all these virtues put on love, which binds them all together in perfect unity. Colossians 3:13-14 (NIV)

In May 2002, my baby sister called to tell me of a schoolmate's sudden death. This particular schoolmate, Lisa Harris-Noble, was a vivacious, loving woman. She lived her life to the fullest, befriended many and always had a smile on her face. The alarming news of her death pierced like a knife and forced me into reflection. The pain of not recalling every precious memory with her penetrated my heart. As we grow older and priorities shift, the reality is that we tend to minimize significant memories that shaped us into what we are today. Life and death awakens the sleeping giant.

My family had a near death experience when I was about ten years old. We were on our way to Toledo, Ohio from Elyria to visit our stepbrothers and sisters. Daddy pulled into Shell Gas Station at the corner of West River and Broad Street. He left the car turned on in park and went inside to pay for the gas. While seated on Mama's lap in the front seat, my baby sister accidentally knocked the gearshift into reverse. The car started to roll backwards and poor Mama, bless her heart, didn't know the first, middle or last thing about cars. A river embankment was directly behind us. Daddy walked out the store, saw the car rolling backwards with his wife and a slew of his children in it, and sprinted towards us. From the back seat, my older brother leaped over the front seat and pressed the break pedal with his hand. When Daddy finally reached the car, he was shakin' like a leaf and said, "Boy, Boy, Boy - I almost lost my family."

At the time of Lisa's death, I lived in Hawaii, but felt the strongest need to attend the funeral. I made travel arrangements and called my favorite cousin to tell her of my plans to fly into Columbus, Ohio. When I arrived, Cuz met me at the airport and we drove to Elyria to attend the wake. We wrestled with the past and sang Minnie Ripperton's, "I stumbled over this photograph, it kind of made me laugh – back down memory lane." On our way to Elyria, ole' school jams played on the radio and we harmonized the lyrics of our favorite tunes.

For all you ole' schoolers, some of the songs that played on the radio were, The Chi-lites, "Toby", Earth, Wind & Fire, "Keep your Head to the Sky", The Funkadelics with George Clinton, "One Nation Under the Groove," and last, but certainly not least, the late Luther Vandross and Cheryl Lynn, "If this World were Mine." Ole school jams were appropriate for the occasion because music had a message "back in the day."

Lisa's death sent us a message - her death symbolized our lives. We searched deep within ourselves to recall fond memories of the past. Cuz and I sang our favorite song from our "play" dance group by High Inergy, "You can't turn me off, in the middle of turnin' me on." We were in total shock and our emotions shifted from laughter to tears. The devastation of her passing had such a profound effect on both of us and we could barely face the reality that she was dead. The closer we got to Elyria, the more we contemplated if we should attend the wake and funeral. Upon arriving we couldn't find a parking space because cars were literally parked everywhere. Cuz found a parking spot in front of the church and we quickly regained our composure before going inside.

People gathered like ants in the church foyer; the lines extended outside. Many thoughts came to mind as we perused the crowd and gracefully took our respective places. Familiar faces filled the church and we saw friends and acquaintances that we hadn't seen in over twenty years. Where did the time go? We were having our high school reunion at Lisa's wake. Sadly, our ten-year reunion didn't consist of this many familiar faces. In every corner of the church people embraced one another and cried for strength in the midst of the storm. We reminisced on days of old and comforted one another through God's grace. My cousin and I greeted nearly fifty people before we reached the casket. As we approached it, a horrific sadness came upon us and the reality of her death overwhelmed us.

In our state of weakness, we hurried past the casket and rushed through the side door. I asked a woman in the hallway of the whereabouts of Lisa's sister, my dear friend Shelley. Lisa and I played basketball together throughout our high school years, but I was much closer to her sister. Suddenly, I recognized her familiar frame near the back door. When our eyes met, tears began to stream down our cheeks. We opened our arms wide toward one another and embraced tearfully. You couldn't have slid a piece of paper between us. We strengthened each other silently and the presence of God was evident. My dear friend suggested that we make plans to spend some time together after the funeral.

On **the Way** to my seat, I glanced at Kyla, Lisa's first cousin and she reached out her hand to me. As I hugged her on the second pew, she appeared shocked by my presence. We were old school friends and she couldn't believe I flew all the Way from Hawaii to attend the funeral. She was with Lisa at her bedside when she passed away. Slowly, she recalled the vivid details of her death as I earnestly listened. I provided words of comfort and peace that only God could have given me.

God will give you the peace that surpasses all understanding when you need it most, if you seek Him. Thoughts of happiness and sadness went through my mind, but survival was the name of the game, at least for the moment. God will not put more on you than you can bear and the wake was confirmation.

After the wake, Cuz and I stopped by to visit with Lisa's mom to show our respect. Upon departure, we remained silenced by the day's occurrences. I longed for shelter from this sudden storm and anticipated the serenity of Mama's house. When I arrived, I subconsciously tried to recapture the moment and mentally prepared myself for the funeral the next day. The following morning, I awoke early to spend time with God. I needed His daily bread.

I pressed my way as I rested in His bosom and drove to the funeral. When I arrived, the doors of the church were already open. I saw a schoolmate I hadn't seen in almost fifteen years and we conversed briefly. He asked, "Girl, what are you doing in town all the Way from Hawaii?" I replied, "She was family; I'm right where I'm supposed to be." People were unaware of my travels because her death was so sudden. I departed Hawaii on Monday morning to attend the wake on Tuesday night. My telephonic communications were restricted to a need-to-know basis. Only my family members knew I was in town.

I 'memba we grew up with extended families. Everybody knew each other and your kinfolk, too. If you clowned in public, it was common practice for a neighborhood mom to confront you on the spot. The confrontation embarrassed you to a certain extent; however, the threat to call your parents was the real issue. More often than not, your behavior would beat you home. As soon as you got home, Mama asked, "What you been doin'?" You wanted to reply, "Is that a trick question, Mama." Right then you knew that the neighborhood mom delivered on her promise. Your fate was in Mama's hands along with the belt or the switch. We didn't have a choice as to what punishment we received. One thing was for certain, we would be punished.

You didn't choose whether you had an extended family or not because it was an extension of your biological family. It consisted of friends, friend's family, a friend of a friend's family, neighbors, neighbor's family, neighbor's friends and so on and so forth. The benefit of an extended family was accountability for your actions, wherever you were. The accountability made you a more responsible, respectable person. Today, we've drifted away from the extended family concept and have become nuclear. The nuclear family primarily consists of the immediate family within your household. Today most families can't account for what goes on within the confines of their own four walls. Sadly, most people don't know the name of the family next door. Is there any wonder why we've lost our sense of family? It takes more than a village to raise a child; we need to get back to the basics and train children up in the fear and admonition of the Lord.

Getting back to the funeral, Lisa's processional was approximately five to six miles long. We followed the car immediately in front of us. Unfortunately, since we are from a big family, Cuz and I have attended many funerals. Cuz said, "It seems like it always rains at funerals." I replied in a somber voice, "God is crying, too."

People often requested Daddy to sing at funerals and churches. I loved to hear him sing my favorite song "99 ½". Before singing, he cleared his throat and said, *"Bear with me--I'm a little hoarse",* and *then he sang like a hummingbird. After his last note, all his kids said, "That's my Daddy." We wanted everyone to know he belonged to us. Daddy's singing group, The Mighty Redeemers, is on the front cover of Frederick Burton's book, The Black America Series, Cleveland's Gospel Music. They sang together for about forty years and were one of the few who signed with Peacock Records. I willingly listened as his group harmonized "Wew, wew, wew, wew, wew, wew, wew, wew" before they started a song. My Daddy is the only living member of the group.* Thank you **Jesus** for **the Way** you have kept him.

After we departed the cemetery, Cuz and I returned to the church where they served dinner. Collectively, we scanned the crowd in search of ole' school friends and moved from table to table reminiscing on days gone by. Later that night, a group of us reunited at the home of Lisa's mom. We laughed and "talked story", recapturing our past was therapeutic. I laughed until my side literally hurt. We revealed childhood secrets and learned more about each other than any of us had anticipated. Somehow, I became the main topic of discussion as we reflected over our lives. We conversed about boyfriends, girlfriends and matters of the heart.

I've always been intrigued with conditions of the heart. Back in the day, one of my AKA's was Queen of Hearts. I've examined hearts as far back as my elementary years. Reactions and responses to love stimulate my mind. I write poetry through inspiration, out of the abundance of the heart the mouth speaks. I plan to publish the poems in another book, "Meditations of the Heart."

The forced reunion was definitely memorable. Briefly, the innocence of my childhood flashed before me and the little girl in me came out to play. Often times, the realities of life take you through the fiery flames and you lose your zest for life. I vividly recall conversing with a dear friend shortly after the funeral. He talked about his many adversities and blamed everyone, except himself for his current predicament. I encouraged him to look into the mirror and he asked, "Are you implying that I Am the source of all my woes?" I replied, "Only if the shoe fits, my friend."

Reuniting with ole' school friends temporarily took me to my secret place of refuge from the storms of life. We laid our burdens down and tried to surrender all. Lisa was the sacrifice. Our reunion was therapy for many wounded souls. We reminisced, hugged, cried, loved and touched on the innermost conditions of our hearts. We breathed life back into each other. I imagine many of us wondered, "And where do we go from here?"

Lisa's sister said it plainly, "I demand for us to keep in closer touch with one another. We shouldn't have allowed ourselves to become so estranged." Some of us knew each other practically all our lives. What a deep sense of history and friendship we shared. Sadly, the little girls and boys that came out to play had to return to their restrictive lifestyles. For the time being, we preferred to be kids again.

"It's wonderful to experience love unconditionally. Unconditional love is freedom from bondage."

HE WHO HAS EARS LET HIM HEAR:
Sudden death awakens you. It makes you think of the significance of each day. Life is not as predictable as we tend to believe. Death enlightens us of the realization of our vulnerabilities. We rationalize the good, the bad, and the ugly. Accept the fact that God is the only one in control at all times. Forgive and love one another in life because if you wait until death it is too late. Death is not only physical, but we must die daily to live a godly life. God is ever-present, we need to reunite and not allow the cares of this world to separate us from God or one another.

Chapter 10

THE FAVOR OF GOD

FIFTH DAY IN THE FIRE: Monday, February 12, 2007

SCRIPTURE FOR THE DAY: In his distress he sought the favor of the **Lord** his **God** and humbled himself greatly before the **God** of his Fathers. 2 Ch 33:12 (NIV)

    I got out of bed around 5:30 a.m., showered, went to Physical Therapy, then to work. I dwelled in the shadow of **the Almighty** and His provision was evident as I continued to press my way. At lunchtime, my pregnant coworker asked if I wanted something to eat and I said, "Yes." About an hour later, she delivered my food; I ate and immediately felt sick. I got up from my desk to try to walk it off. As I held onto the stair rail, the control of my body escaped me. My body no longer obeyed my mind. I fought hard not to vomit in the hallway and asked the **Lord** to keep me. He answered my prayer and I made it to the restroom. I vomited several times and was glad no one else was in the restroom. I wiped my face with a cold paper towel and began to feel better. I returned to my office and continued to be tested. A few minutes later, I went upstairs and started to feel sick again. Once again, I called on the **Lord** and he answered. I made it to the restroom and the pain overpowered me. I vomited again and the chills permeated my body. The Lieutenant that I worked with heard me and said, "Chief, are you OK?" I said, "I **Am** sick." She asked, "Do you need me to do anything for you?" and I replied, "No, I just need to get well."

I concentrated on my health, returned to my office and immediately called central appointments. The operator asked me to explain "my condition" and followed up with "The nurse will return your call shortly." I finished a few tasks. The nurse called, I explained my symptoms and she said, "We don't have any appointments, but I'll squeeze you in, can you get over here in fifteen minutes?" I replied, "I'm on my way." I thanked **God** for His favor, informed the Captain that I had a short notice doctor's appointment and left.

When I arrived, my sister-in-**Christ**, a member of my church, was at the counter and asked, "Chief, are you alright? I said, "No, I **Am** sick." She said, "Follow me" and escorted me to a room to check my vital signs. After she took my blood pressure, she asked what else she could do for me and I requested a bed to lie in. She led me to an empty room, on **the Way** she told someone I was her Chief and she was about to take care of me. We entered the room and she said, "Lie down Chief, the doctor will be here in a minute. Let me get you a warm blanket." She covered me and left quietly. **Lord** knows I needed a secret place to hide from this terrible storm.

God gave me a secret place during my school years, "my home away from home" at my Angel's, Ms. Mary Helen's, AKA Mother to her children. Her house closely resembled The Cosby's and she cared for me as if I was one of her own. Mother's heart was made of gold and she continually gave. On several occasions, I walked past her bedroom and heard her praying in tongues. I meditated on the words she prayed. One day I asked her whom she talked to and what she said. She explained how she talked to God and the power you have when you speak in tongues. My Angel taught me about the Holy Spirit and not to fear the gift of speaking in tongues. I learned to give without expectation. The Bible says in Luke 6:38 (NIV), "Give and it will be given unto you. A good measure, pressed down, shaken together and running over, will be poured into your lap. For with the measure you use, it will be measured to you."

When the doctor entered, I described my symptoms and told him I needed some "scripts." He diagnosed me with Acute Bronchitis, put my prescription for antibiotics in the computer, and asked if I needed one or two days off. I said it didn't matter, he gave me a quarter's slip and I left.

When I left, my sister-in-Christ passed me in the hallway and pulled me into a room where she proceeded to give me special treatment. I wanted desperately to leave, but she desired to lift my burden. Her spirit of servanthood consumed her and I appreciated my sister being my keeper. She told me to go directly to the pharmacy and tell the receptionist that my prescription was already in the system to speed up the process. I thanked her and said goodbye.

I went to the counter, told the receptionist who I was and she checked the system. She said my prescription wasn't in the system yet. I asked if she was certain and she replied, "Yes, you need to get a ticket and go to counter #1." I smiled and walked over to get an active duty ticket because I was in uniform and uniformed personnel received the highest priority. I turned in my ticket and the woman said, "Chief, please have a seat, someone will be with you shortly." I sat in the chair, curled up my legs, and tried to rest. I leaned my head back, looked up, and closed my eyes. I had a headache and the slightest whisper sounded like a freight train. The pain oozed through my entire body. I didn't have to wait long for them to call my number and when they did, I went to the counter. The woman said, "Chief, please sign here." I signed, thanked her and went to admissions to turn in my quarters slip.

Afterwards, I walked to my car perfectly aware of the fact that I was too sick to drive home. I turned on my Christian music and prayed for **the Lord** to drive me home safely. I started on my journey and almost pulled off to the side of the road several times. I had urges to vomit the entire trip. Approximately three-five minutes from home, I could barely keep the vomit down. I kept praying to **God** for favor and He answered my prayer, once again.

When I made it home, I thanked **God** for answered prayer, hurried out of my clothes and crawled into bed. I felt miserable when my husband came home and asked if I was awake. I could barely speak and replied, "Yes, I can't sleep; I haven't slept since last Wednesday night." He looked at me astonished. When night came and everyone had retired to bed, I had given up on sleep. I got my mink blanket, went to the living room, took the decorative pillows off the oversized-chair, tossed them on the floor and curled up in it. I got up and went to the garage for a bucket to put beside my chair. I needed a remedy to restore my voice and went into the kitchen, cut some lemon, boiled it in water, and made a hot tonic with honey.

I sipped my tonic on the way back to the living room and propped myself in the chair. I sat upright and began to "talk story" with **God**. My husband entered and asked if I needed anything. I said, "Yes, a pillow to put under my feet, please." He got one, tucked it gently under my feet and asked if I needed anything else. I replied, "I'm sorry to bother you, but can you please bring me one more pillow to rest my head on?" I tried to get comfortable in the chair, but couldn't. Every angle I turned was one of discomfort.

He brought me the pillow and said, "Don't ever think you're a bother to me; I'm here to serve you." I replied, "Thanks, I love you" and he left. For about an hour, I didn't cough much and began to think, "I'm finally going to get some sleep!" Restoration was finally here and I was ready to dance like David, but sleep never came. I coughed and spat, coughed and spat worse than I ever heard Papa. The purging continued because my test wasn't over. I shook my head, got up, and read my Bible.

HE WHO HAS EARS LET HIM HEAR:

The favor of God is awesome. The Spirit dwells in us and intercedes for us when we call out to Him. The Holy Spirit rewards us with spiritual gifts and His favor is everlasting. Jesus desires to have a relationship with us. Get to know Him for yourself. When sickness and disease come against you, seek His face and pray for favor. God allows us to grow in favor with Him and with men. Is your name written in the book of Life? Do you know Jesus? Avail yourself of God and be purged of all that is not of Him. Purging is a form of deliverance. When you walk in the image of God, favor is more abundant.

Chapter 11

OBEDIENCE

Does the Lord delight in burnt offerings and sacrifices as much as in obeying the voice of the Lord? To obey is better than sacrifice and to heed is better than the fat of rams.
1 Samuel 15:22 (NIV)

The promises of God are "Yes" and "Amen" and we are heirs of His promise. In 1999, my family and I received military orders to Hawaii. From the onset, I knew the assignment was in accordance with God's perfect plan. After we arrived in Hawaii, God reminded us of His promise and His rainbows perched over the mountains were heavenly. In Genesis 9:12-16 (NIV) God said, "This is the sign of the covenant I Am making between me and you and every living creature with you, a covenant for all generations to come: I have set my rainbows in the clouds, and it will be a sign of the covenant between me and the earth. Whenever I bring clouds over the earth and the rainbow appears in the clouds, I will remember my covenant between me and you and all living creatures of every kind. Never again will the waters become a flood to destroy all life. Whenever the rainbow appears in the clouds, I will see it and remember the everlasting covenant between God and all living creatures of every kind on the earth."

The rainbows were memorable and I recalled times of praying and fasting. When alone on **the Way** home, as I approached the "7" mile marker to the city of Kapolei, I turned off my music and prayed aloud to **God**. Hawaii was truly paradise, my earthly supply of milk and honey. **God** revealed heaven on earth through His glorious creations – **the Spirit** of Aloha, orchards, vineyards, gardens, flowers, plants, pineapples, fruit trees, rainbows, mountains, blue skies, beautiful beaches and sand. The Hawaiians refer to conversing as "talk-story."

In Hawaii, **God** revealed His healing power through my firstborn son on the third day of my fast. Day one and day two of the fast were uneventful. On day three upon arriving home, I asked my husband where our firstborn son was and he replied, "He's in bed sick; he's been there since he came from school." I ran upstairs, touched his hot body, placed my hand on his forehead and prayed to **God** to heal our son. He turned cold instantly and I rejoiced in **the Lord** and returned downstairs. My husband asked, "How is he?" and I replied, "He is well." I started feeling a piercing pain in my stomach and went to the restroom with my Bible in hand. The devil tried to steal my joy, sickness latched on to my body and I began to vomit repeatedly. The pain intensified and permeated my entire body. I knew to resist the devil and called on the name of **Jesus.** The devil fled because of my resistance. **God** rescued me from the hand of the enemy. I rejoiced in the **Lord**, opened and closed the door behind me, and counted it all joy according to His purpose.

Later that night, I went to the upper room and asked **the Holy Spirit** to reveal my true purpose. The Bible says in Acts 2:17 (NIV), "In the last days, **God** says, I will pour out my **Spirit** on all people. Your sons and daughters will prophesy, your young men will see visions, your old men will dream dreams. Even on my servants, both men and women, I will pour out my **Spirit** in those days, and they will prophesy. I will show wonders in the heaven above and signs on the earth below, blood and fire and billows of smoke. The sun will be turned to darkness and the moon to blood before the coming of the great and glorious day of the Lord. And everyone who calls on the name of the Lord will be saved." The next morning, the Holy Spirit whispered in a gentle voice for me to continue the fast. There was more that He required of me and I obeyed His command. While at work, my other-mother, Ma Mazie called to "talk story" and shared her testimony of how God healed her sickness and disease. I thanked God for His healing hand and said, "Lord, by your stripes, I Am healed." I praised God for His goodness and tender mercy.

Shortly thereafter, my sister-in-Christ, who received salvation the same day I did, called and prayed for me in her prayer language the entire time. God charged His Angel over me and she covered me in prayer. After work, I drove home rejoicing in the Lord. At night, I went to the upper room to pray. The Holy Spirit led me to fast again the following day. I obeyed the voice of God and said, "Lord, wherever You want me to go, I'll go and whatever You want me to do, I'll do."

While at work the next morning, one of the base chaplains called to compliment me on my voice message. He said, "I can tell by the sound of your voice that you're a Christian, your message truly blessed me. Sometimes, I call just to hear your voice and to be encouraged." I thanked him and gave God all the glory.

I stayed encouraged. After work, I went by the caretakers to pick up my youngest son. Upon my arrival, she exclaimed, "I have something to tell you! When I went to the commissary today, a man approached your son and me. He looked like a man of God and asked, 'Whose son is that?' I said, 'That's my friend Helen's son. Why do you want to know?' He said, 'You tell his mother to take extra good care of him; he is a Pastor.' He followed me around the entire store and prophesied over him and kept saying, 'He is a

Pastor; take good care of him.' Before I realized it, he was gone. He must have been an Angel."

I embraced my son, The Pastor and thanked God. I looked him in his eyes and confessed, "You're blessed and highly favored in the Lord." I drove home excited and shared the information with my husband. I continued to rejoice in His goodness and the Holy Spirit led me to eat. I went to the upper room and continued to pray and said, "No weapon formed against me and my family shall ever prosper." The gift of God is eternal life and I thanked Him for His loving-kindness and tender mercies.

My oldest sister was my gift from God in the form of Mama #2. She left her earthly body on Good Friday, "7" years ago. The roller-coaster ride started on December 31, 1999 (New Year's Eve). Mama #2 called me from Virginia to "talk story" about her plans for the evening. We had a lovely hour-long discussion and hung up. Approximately two hours later, I received a call from my niece that they had to rush Mama #2 to the emergency room. The information floored me and I called my sister-in- Christ in Virginia to ask for a favor. I explained my situation and asked if she would go by the hospital to check on my family, she replied, "Sure, sweetie." I said, "If I need to be on the next plane 'smoking' just say the Word." She called back about thirty minutes later and relayed the message, "Come, as soon as you can."

The words, "Come as soon as you can," echoed in my mind. I nursed my three-week-old son and asked the Lord, "What shall I do?" He answered, I packed my bags and my youngest son and I caught the next plane to Virginia. I left my firstborn son in Hawaii with my husband. Do you remember all the hype about flights on December 31, 1999? I put my trust in God and feared not. My plane arrived in Norfolk around 10:30 p.m., that night.

Upon arrival, my brother met us at the airport and we went straight to the hospital. Mama #2 had open-heart surgery on January 2, 2000. After surgery, she was extremely weak. My family assembled and prayed. My sisters-in-**Christ** and other-father, Mr. "G" covered me from the storm. I returned to Hawaii after about a week's stay. **The Physician** discharged her several weeks later.

In mid-March, my niece contacted me to tell me that Mama #2 was back in the hospital and her prognosis wasn't good. I flew to Virginia, this time with my firstborn son. I no longer nursed my youngest son and left him in Hawaii with my husband. We went straight to the hospital upon arrival. Based on the seriousness of her condition, they prohibited children from entry. I desperately wanted my son to see my sister. In 1995, Mama #2 and her newly married husband moved to Virginia, from Ohio, to live with my husband and me. At the time, I was pregnant with my firstborn son and my sister witnessed the entire pregnancy. Mama #2 and my firstborn son formed a special bond and I wanted them to see one another.

My sister needed another open-heart surgery. Her body was still relatively weak from the first surgery. The night before I departed Hawaii, four of my sisters-in-**Christ** discerned I was in the fire. We called upon the name of **Jesus** and He was in our midst. My sisters covered me and interceded in **the Holy Spirit**. I wrote the experience in a notebook:

"**Lord Jesus**, You showed up and I declare You were **Wonderful**. The sisters marveled in Your goodness and Your **Holy Ghost** power was supreme. You healed broken hearts and delivered us from the hands of the enemy. You left a **Sovereign** peace upon the household that only You could do. Blessed be the name of the **Lord**, blessed by the name of the **Lord**." On March

24, 2000, my firstborn and I prepared for our departure back to Hawaii. The devil tried his best to destroy what God blessed.

My firstborn and I drove to my niece's house to pick up Mama. The devil tried me as my firstborn son became ill. As we waited for the stoplight to turn green my son said, "Mommy, I'm sick." I reached over the seat, emptied the contents from a Mary Kay bag, handed it to him and said, "Throw up in this." I proceeded to place one hand on his forehead and drove with the other. I cited this prayer: "Father, in the precious and mighty name of Jesus, I ask that You will once again show up and allow Your healing power to rule over this situation. Heal my son and take away this sickness in Your son Jesus' name."

At the hospital, the nurses prepped my sister in the Intensive Care Unit. I waited patiently for them to inform me of when to enter. Before entry, I washed my hands, and then put on the sterile gloves and gown. I spoke healing words to my sister. Her nurse was kind and considerate; she kept me informed daily of my sister's condition. I had a special request and explained it to her. I asked, "May I please bring my son through the back entrance to see my sister before we depart for Hawaii?" God had already prepared her heart, along with another nurse. She granted me the desire of my heart and they escorted me through a staff only entrance.

We went to the wait area to get Mama and my firstborn son and then entered through the back door. My son stood several feet away from Mama #2's bedside and whispered, "Auntie." With all the strength in her feeble body, she raised her head high and my sister's light shined brighter than anything I had ever witnessed. I saw an Angel. I smiled and began to cry; she smiled back at me. My son and I told her how much we loved her. We exchanged a few more words and I refused to say good-bye because I knew I would see my Angel again in heaven. That was the last time I saw my sister alive in her earthly body. I departed with thanksgiving in my heart and praised God.

The devil tried to steal my praise. I shared with Mama the goodness of God and the Way He showed up the night before. My son began to vomit all over his clothes on the Way from the hospital. The devil is a liar! I remained considerably calm. At my sister-in-Christ's house, I worked vigorously. It appeared as if we ran late for the airport, but I rejoiced in the Holy Spirit. I removed two sets of clothes from the suitcase, ironed them, changed my son's clothes, cleaned out my sister's car, and then sprayed Febreeze in it. I placed three small plastic bags in my coat pocket, along with several cold compresses, and we left for the airport. When we arrived, my sister-in-Christ led the prayer, kissed us and left.

I anticipated the snares of the enemy; I knew Satan was mad. About five minutes before we landed at Dulles Airport in Washington D.C., my son said, "Mommy, I got to throw up." I pulled a bag out of my pocket and said, "Throw up in here." There was a hole in the bottom of the bag. Instantly, I could have chosen to get upset, but I chose not to because the devil wasn't about to steal my joy. I asked my son how he felt, took the cold face rag from his backpack, and placed it on his forehead. His pants and one sock were soaked in vomit, his seat was about three-fourths soaked, but I was in perfect peace. My son and I were the last ones to depart the plane. I explained to the flight attendant that he was ill and apologized for the vomit in his seat. She replied, "That's OK, have a nice day."

God had already purposed the three hour lay over. My son and I went into the restroom; I removed his pants and sock, washed them in the airport sink and then dried them with the restroom hand dryer. After I finished, I still had about an hour left to reflect on the goodness of God. He gave me peace in the midst of the storm because I entered into His presence with thanksgiving. The trip to Hawaii from Dulles was Wonderful and my son was fine. Jesus said to resist the devil and he will flee.

On April 1, 2000, my sister's doctor called and said they didn't expect her to live longer than twenty-four hours. After I got off the phone, I told my husband we needed to pack while I was still in my right mind. After packing, my husband placed the suitcases at the front entrance. I was in the fire the first twenty days of April. Everyday, I prayed faithfully at the "7" mile marker but began to negotiate and reason with God. I was on an emotional rollercoaster. I kept praying for God to heal my sister. I asked Him not to take her because my desire was for her to be a living testimony of His goodness. I begged and pleaded with God in prayer, but always ended with the words, "not my will, but Thy will be done, in Jesus name."

Everyday, for about a week, I stumbled over the packed suitcases. Finally, I said to my husband, "I can't deal with those suitcases any longer; please take them away." We unpacked and I began to pray. I prayed a prayer of faith and made my request known unto God. I specifically asked God for favor. I reminded Jesus that He left this earth on Good Friday and asked, "Lord, if it is Your will to take my sister, please take her on Good Friday and grant me the strength to endure it." On April 21, (Good Friday) at approximately 6:00 a.m., I received a call that my sister died a few minutes earlier. I had found peace that surpassed all understanding, and I found rest in the Word. God granted me specifically what I asked for and I meditated on, "There is no greater love than this and this favor is from the Father, just for you my Daughter." The promises of God are "Yes" and "Amen" and I praised God in the midst of the storm. My family and I packed and then flew to Ohio.

When my family and I arrived at Mama's she was engrossed in burial preparations. My spirit of excellence and servanthood reconnected me to Mommy and Mother Helen. I told Mama to rest and be still as I put on the full armor of God to orchestrate the funeral arrangements. God led the Way and I followed. I heard many conversations about cremation because my sister's insurance had lapsed without our knowledge. I asked my niece if my sister desired cremation and she replied, "No, but she didn't have any insurance." The devil is a liar. A decent burial became priority for Mama #2. I rallied the family and asked everyone how much they planned to give toward her burial. My sister-in-Christ flew from Virginia to be by my side. God charged His Angel over me to cover me in the midst of the storm.

The storms raged the night of her wake and I fainted when I saw her in the casket. My Angel escorted me to Mama's house. The next morning I was beside myself. Before we left for the funeral, my four-year-old firstborn son asked if he could pray and I replied, "yes". He prayed and I rested in his prayer all day long. At the funeral, my firstborn son shouted hallelujah several times as the pastor preached and I rejoiced in God's goodness. We paid the price in full for her burial and buried her in fine linen with beautiful flowers. "I'll see you soon, my sister."

HE WHO HAS EARS LET HIM HEAR:
You have not because you ask not. Make your requests known unto God and be specific. Obedience is better than sacrifice. When you pray, pray for God's perfect will to be done. When the Holy Spirit speaks, obey His commands. God rewards obedience and His promises are "Yes" and "Amen." As a child of God, you have authority and power through the Holy Spirit. Seek divine order and intervention at all times. God is pouring out His Spirit through His miracles, signs, and wonders. You can live in paradise on earth and in heaven. God is faithful.

Chapter 12

SACRIFICE

SIXTH DAY IN THE FIRE: Tuesday, February 13, 2007

SCRIPTURE FOR THE DAY: Through **Jesus**, therefore, let us continually offer to God a sacrifice of praise – the fruit of lips that confess his name. And do not forget to do good and to share with others, for with such sacrifices God is pleased. Hebrews 13:15-16 (NIV)

I got up feeling refreshed, but my back ached from being upright in the oversized-chair practically all night. The temporary pain thunder-bolted on my spine, but I pressed my way onward. I showered, dressed and went to work. When I arrived, the Captain asked, "Chief, what are you doing here?" I replied, "I'm fine, sir." He said, "No you're not. Aren't you on quarters?" I told him not to worry and promised to go home if I felt sick. Later that afternoon, a coworker came into my office and asked how I felt. I whispered in a hoarse voice, "My sickness comes and goes." She replied, "The last time I was sick, my husband made me some chicken soup and it cured me." I replied, "Chicken soup to heal my soul sure sounds good. I think I'll stop by the store on my way home to purchase the ingredients." I worked all day and caught up on a few tasks.

After work, I called home to see if anyone needed anything. My firstborn son asked for Valentine's Day cards and my "7" year old son asked if I could make cupcakes for his class of twelve students. When I went to the store my mind wandered, and I forgot what I went there to purchase. I saw a coworker's husband as he hurried along to purchase flowers for his wife. He said he had procrastinated and I replied, "It's really not important when you purchase the gift, as long as she receives it on Valentine's Day." He slowed down and said, "You're right, have a good night Chief."

I thought long and hard about what I needed to buy. As I walked toward the food section, the aroma from the rotisserie chicken hypnotically lured me to where it was being prepared. I asked the woman behind the counter which one she recommended. She said, "They're all good." I kept my eye on the prize and watched them rotate in the slow cooker. Another woman walked up and I asked her which one she preferred? She replied, "I don't like the hot one or the barbeque, I like the lemon-pepper one the best." I replied, "I'll take one of those." The woman said, "Come back in a few minutes, they aren't done yet." I asked if she would please save one for me and she replied, "Certainly."

I walked around the store a few more minutes and then hurried back for my chicken. I asked the woman behind the counter, "Is it ready yet?" She pointed toward the bottom of the rack and replied, "It's right there, already done." I removed the lemon-peppered chicken from the rack, placed it gently on top of the other items in my cart and kept my eyes planted on it. As I approached the register, a family of four emptied their cart. The little girl smiled at me and I smiled back. Their cart over-flowed with groceries and the woman stared at me, as if to say, "Please be patient with me. I'm almost done." I smiled at her and waited patiently. After they were finished, the cashier rang up my items and I left. I could hardly wait to get home.

I drove home quickly and put away the groceries. My husband had already prepared dinner with the leftover chicken from the day before. I told him that I preferred to eat the one I bought. We fixed the plates; the kids set the table, we prayed, and then ate. I ate small portions and my stomach began to feel weak. I stopped eating and informed my youngest son that it was his responsibility to make the cupcakes, but I offered to assist. After dinner, I methodically cleaned the chicken and prepared chicken soup for my soul.

Back in the day, **the Way** *our family prepared dinner was interesting, to say the least. My older sisters cooked the majority of the time. I didn't have to cook much, but I had to clean the house from top to bottom. I cleaned it religiously and taught my younger siblings how to clean, too. My sisters consistently prepared their favorite meals; one cooked spaghetti or liver, another barbeque chicken and one loved to experiment; when she cooked you never knew what to expect.*

We didn't expect to eat dinner together as a family, not with ten kids in one household. We were hardly ever home at the same time. Amazingly, Mama always knew who didn't eat. Whenever one of her kids came through the door, their first question was "Mama, who didn't eat?" Without hesitation, she answered correctly and you remembered her words as you fixed your plate. When you saw what was for dinner, you automatically knew which sister cooked. If you were the last one to eat, you could help yourself to what was leftover. Back in the day, we appreciated leftovers and enjoyed them to the fullest. "Waste not, want not" is what Mama used to say. I get a tadbit over-cooked when someone says, "I don't eat leftovers." Yeah, whatever!

I asked my "7" year old son which cake mix he preferred, lemon or white. He replied, "I'll take the white one, Mommy."

He reminded me that we needed to make enough cupcakes for twelve students and wanted to know if there was enough for his Teacher to have one. I said, "Sure we have more than enough." He read the instructions and informed us that we needed a bowl, water, oil and eggs. I told him to put the water in the measuring cup. I got the oil from underneath the stove and my firstborn son removed the eggs from the refrigerator. I cracked the eggs against the bowl and my youngest son asked, "Why do you crack them on the bowl?" I explained that it didn't matter how you cracked them, as long as you don't get shell fragments in your mix. My sons poured the cupcakes in the baking pan and placed them in the oven to bake.

I turned on the oven light so he could watch them rise, set the timer and instructed my "7" year old son to watch them. I told my sons not to jump near the oven or the cupcakes would fall. As a child, my youngest son spoke like a child and asked, "Why?" I explained the difference between a fallen and a risen cake. He smiled in excitement as if he understood. When the timer went off, I removed the cupcakes, placed them on the cooling rack, loosened the sides with a knife, and complemented my sons on a job well done.

They were eager to frost the cupcakes. My "7" year old son asked if we had enough for him and his brother to have one. I replied, "Yes, there's plenty." I reminded them to sign their Valentine's Day cards. I laughed and said, "I forgot to buy the cards." My sons begged me to go back to the store. I humbly agreed because it was my fault that I allowed the lemon-peppered chicken to distract me.

I placed the second batch of cupcakes in the oven, turned on the timer and asked my husband to keep an eye on them. My sons cleaned the bowl and licked the spoon before I drove back to the grocery store. When I got to the store, I was determined not to buy anything more than the cards. However, I bought chicken broth for the soup (smile). A few minutes later, I returned home and my sons rejoiced. They filled out the cards and I reminded them of their bedtime. I wiped off the table and got a container for the cupcakes. My husband examined it and asked why I was using the nice container. I explained it was durable and easy for our son to carry and he nodded his head in agreement.

I showed my son the proper way to carry the container on the bus and encouraged him not to worry. I reminded him of how responsible he was and assured him that he would be fine. We kissed our sons goodnight and they went to bed. I placed the extra cupcakes in a separate container, washed the dishes, swept the kitchen, signed my husband's Valentine's Day card, placed it in his cap and went to bed. All night I coughed, spat, coughed and spat like Papa. I couldn't sleep, so I got up and read my Bible.

HE WHO HAS EARS LET HIM HEAR:
Our children are a gift from God. Train up children in the way they should go, God will finish what you have started. In our weakness, the grace of God is sufficient. Praise Him while you're going through tribulations. We have to decrease for God to increase. Jesus was the sacrificial Lamb and He died so we would have life more abundantly. He paid the price in full once and for all. God gives us a perfect will to choose. Lay your burdens down and tend to the needs of others. It's not about you! Give God your best and share with others. Love God and reaffirm His greatness. Speak life.

Chapter 13

THE DEVIL IS A LIAR

Submit yourselves, then, to God. Resist the devil, and he will flee from you. Come near to God and He will come near to you. James 4:7-8 (NIV)

Each of us has a story to tell. When we "talk-story" it unravels us and removes layers. We come to realize that we're more alike, than different. God made each of us in His image, but we were born into the sinful nature of this world. God has given unto each of us a measure of faith. Exercise your faith and speak to the mountain. My grandfather, Daddy Nelson's sister, Mabel Davis, the matriarch of the Nelson family, spoke these words of wisdom at the 2007 Nelson Family Reunion, "I Am climbing up the mountain, because we are not here to stay and some of you I may never see again, until Judgment Day."

Jesus is the only one who knows how much dirt is on your mountain and how many mountains you've had to climb. It matters most that the grace of God is sufficient and that the devil is a liar. The devil comes to steal, kill, and destroy. He'll use anyone, even family members to accomplish his plan. He used my sister-in-Christ's biological Father as his messenger to destroy the intended purpose **God** had predestined for her life. **God** inspired her to "talk-story." This is her story:

"I 'memba when I was an innocent five-year-old little girl. Mr. Goody-Man stole my voice, self-esteem and identity. He was an authority figure, a close friend of the family. His plan was to entice me based on my desires. As a child, I desired the sweeter things in life like candy and gum. Whenever I was in his presence, he used to say, 'It's in my pocket' and I reached into his pocket for my goodies. Through his manipulation and deceit, he taught me 'quid pro quo' (something for something) at an early age. If I allowed him to touch me (pats and hugs) and promised not to tell, I received 'goodies' in return.

He consistently provided goodies and planted seeds of doubt, unworthiness, self-pity and all the negative things that kept me in bondage. Around the age of twelve, I learned that Mr. Goody-Man was my biological **Father**. When the truth came out, nothing changed, his heart remained hardened and he continued to be Mr. Goody-Man. I had a spirit of fear over me and was frequently afraid to get out of bed at night to use the restroom; I wet the bed well into my preteen years. In my youthful days, I loved to play sports; however, transportation was limited and I relied heavily on Mr. Goody-Man to transport me and sometimes my friends, to and from sporting events. I became dependent on him and started to blame myself. I manipulated the situation in my teen years; the name of the game was survival.

I survived the only way I knew how. The stronghold of Mr. Goody-Man's lies and accusations grew into weeds that almost choked the life out of me. Like a shadow of darkness, he followed me places. As long as I let him touch me, he was happy and rewarded my behavior with money and other things my mother couldn't afford. Mr. Goody-Man used to say, 'No other boy or man will ever love you like I do. I'm the only one who understands you.' Death and life are in the power of the tongue and he spoke death to me at an early age. His words pierced like a knife. I thought in order to protect myself and those I loved, I had to keep Mr. Goody-Man's curse a secret.

As a child and young adult, the secrets haunted me. I sought after love in emotionally and physically abusive relationships. I thought abuse was normal. I relied on others to make me whole. This horrible secret nearly killed me. I often think what my life might have been like if I would have "talked-story" and revealed the secret to my mother or sister. My mother went to her grave never knowing my secret.

I Am revealing my story so that others who are bound by their past will be set free. I was a victim and as a child, I responded as a child. The devil is a liar. In 2001, I received my 'spiritual mother' and prayer warrior. Although she never bore a child of her own, she carried me in the depths of her belly. I've been going through a 'rebirthing' ever since. The more I unraveled my secrets to my prayer warrior, the more saints interceded for me.

The prayers of the righteous availed much. At the age of thirty-nine, I looked in the mirror and saw myself made in His image. This was the beginning of my ongoing recovery process. I entered into counseling and joined a support group for abuse. I learned that not all abuse leaves visible marks. In the beginning stages, my pride almost destroyed me. I lied to the counselors because I was used to pretending and covering up the Truth. The devil is a liar. When I began to tell the Truth, the burdens began to lift.

Jesus is the burden-bearer and because of my salvation, I had to forgive Mr. Goody-Man in order for me to be free. The Bible says in Luke 6:37 (ESV), 'Judge not, and you will not be judged;

condemn not, and you will not be condemned; forgive, and you will be forgiven.' When I had a child of my own, I was determined to break the chains of this generational curse. I confronted him; unfortunately, he died the same way he lived, with a hardened heart and no remorse. His wages of sin lead to death. On Judgment Day, each of us will have to give account for our deeds.

I speak blessings over my family. The generational curse has been broken. My children are blessed and highly favored in the Lord. By His stripes, I Am healed. Mr. Goody-Man is not a single-entity; he was a thorn in my life and possibly yours. He was a part of the script that the devil had written for my life. The devil is a liar. I'm no longer bound or lost. Jesus broke the chains and His blood set me free. Thank God, for the Angels He charged over me and for loving me enough to protect me. I thank God that somebody prayed for me.

Prayers cover you in the storms. I've been in the fire most of my life, but praise God for his grace and mercy. In spite of the devil's tactics, the hand of God protected me. I Am a living testimony of the goodness of God. I could have been dead, sleeping in my grave, but God isn't finished with me yet. For such a time as this, the Lord recently revealed that He has washed away my sins and has set me free. The devil tried desperately to destroy me at an early age because I'm the apple of God's eye. The devil is a liar." Romans 16:20 (NIV) says, "The God of peace will soon crush Satan under your feet."

HE WHO HAS EARS, LET HIM HEAR:
The devil is a liar. Uproot the root of issues; if you don't the issues will continue to grow. We all have seeds that need to be uprooted. The weeds (Satan) have choked us. The enemy can be so deeply rooted that it destroys "the inner me." Rebuke the devil when he says no one understands you better than him. God made you in

His image and no one knows or understands you better than Him. The snares of the enemy are a form of bondage and entrapment. Sometimes healing comes from confrontation; past wounds need to be exposed. Exposure can lead to closure. Pride comes before the fall. If you desire wholeness, touch the hem of His garment. Jesus was wounded for our transgressions and pierced for our iniquities. He paid the price so you wouldn't have to. Be healed. Don't let the evil secrets that the devil planted to enslave you; seek to understand the secrets of the Kingdom of Heaven. With God, all things are possible.

Chapter 14

THE WEDDING FEAST

"7TH" DAY IN THE FIRE: Wednesday, February 14, 2007 (Valentine's Day)

SCRIPTURE FOR THE DAY: Blessed is the man who will eat at the feast in the kingdom of God. Luke 14:15 (NIV)

Another day in the fire, I didn't sleep all night. My husband and I got out of bed and wished each other a Happy Valentine's Day. After we dressed, he led the prayer, kissed me and said, "I'll see you later, have a nice day." I drove to Physical Therapy and upon entering, wished everyone a Happy Valentine's Day.

After therapy, I went to work. My office was empty and there was a sign on the door that read: We'll be back at 12:00. I erased the board, went into my office and transferred the Valentine's Day confetti from its original container to a cup. I went to each office, passed out Hershey's Chocolate Kisses, sprinkled confetti on the desks and wished everyone a Happy Valentine's Day. When I returned to my office, my husband phoned to thank me for his gift and said, "Your friend, Chief Jackson delivered them and she

87

said to tell you hello." I responded, "Wow, isn't that lovely, I guess if anyone had to be **the Deliverer** then why not let it be my friend." He said he loved me and hung up.

My stomach was still weak, but I felt like I needed to eat something. I reheated the homemade chicken soup in the microwave. My pregnant coworker smelled it, asked what it was and I replied, "Homemade chicken soup for my soul. I made it last night, but didn't bring in enough to share." She replied, "Well it sure smells good, Chief." I told her I would bring her some in tomorrow.

Mid-afternoon, the base florist delivered a dozen red and yellow roses to my office. I called my husband to thank him and he asked what words were on the card. I replied, "I'm too busy admiring the beautiful flowers, I haven't opened the card yet." I read the card to him: "Happy Valentine's Day from the man in your life." He said, "It was supposed to say from the men in your life." I said, "Oh my, all the men in my life want to wish me a Happy Valentine's Day" and he replied, "Yes."

After work, I rushed home for the Valentine's Day Banquet at the church. When I got home, I asked my husband what he had planned to wear, and he said he wasn't sure. I selected my outfit from the closet in the guest room and returned to my bedroom. I examined my husband's attire and suggested that he wear a new shirt as opposed to the old, faded one he had chosen. He willingly agreed.

Shortly thereafter, the doorbell rang and it was the babysitter, my friend the Chief. We "talked story" and I thanked her for delivering the flowers to my husband earlier. I told her to help herself to anything in the refrigerator, but to give the leftovers to our sons. My youngest insisted he needed to eat something else, but his **Father** said to eat the leftovers. He wept and his **Father** took him aside to explain why he needed to eat the leftovers before they spoiled. My son understood and nodded his head in agreement. I reminded Chief to have our sons bathe and complete their homework. She replied, "I got this and don't worry about the time." We hugged her, loved on our sons and left.

My husband and I pulled into the church parking lot and greeted a couple as the woman helped her husband with his tie. As we entered the fellowship hall, the ambience was heavenly. Everything was in perfect order and divinely orchestrated. The banquet was like a wedding celebration. Multi-colored balloons circulated the room; in the front was a beautifully decorated arch that resembled the beautiful rainbows I saw regularly in Hawaii. There was a majestically adorned table to the right, fit for royalty. The elder and ministers took their respective places at the head table.

An usher escorted us to a table already prepared for us. We looked around the room and waved happily to the saints. One of the ministers blessed the food and instructed the men to serve the women. The women smiled in expectation. The aroma of the meal was sensational. My husband served me, fixed his plate, took his seat to the right of me and then asked if the meat tasted good. I replied, "It's delicious" and he tasted it and agreed. I asked him if he wanted my bread and he answered, "Yes, put it on my plate and I'll eat it."

After supper, we were entertained. One couple emceed and told jokes as we laughed at their humor. The first dance group performed magnificently. Afterwards, a mother and daughter ensemble danced beautifully to a more contemporary selection. Everyone applauded and celebrated their talents. An usher came to our table and said, "Desserts are in the back, help yourself." My husband chose pastries and strawberries for our enjoyment;

I ignored the pastries and planted my eyes on the beautiful strawberries. I asked my husband if he wanted some of the strawberries and he said I could have all of them. As I anticipated, they were sweeter than honey.

I savored the taste of the strawberries. After dessert, we gave thanks. Husbands thanked wives for being their helpmates. Wives thanked husbands for being their covering and protection. A woman thanked God in advance for the husband He would send to her one day. Another woman thanked the chair beside her, she said her husband was sitting there, but no one could see him. I thanked God for sisterhood and for my sisters-in-Christ who have loved me unconditionally.

After thanksgiving, husbands gave wives various gifts. The single woman beside me said, "I was promised a gift." I replied, "And so it shall be" then reached into my purse and handed her some perfumed lotion. With a "kool-aid" smile she replied, "Thank you." Next, they called the men on stage and the women continued admiring their gifts. The hostess instructed the women to assemble on the floor, a step beneath the men. The Teacher taught us the dance we were to perform in the presence of the King. We practiced our parts in excitement. After rehearsal, the husbands stepped off the stage with outstretched arms to dance with their wives. In submission, the wives extended their hands toward them. Single men and women danced together. Everyone rejoiced. Lastly, we humbly embraced one another, said goodbye and departed for home.

When we got home, I desired to "talk story" about the heavenly banquet. The Chief was sleeping on the couch. I awakened her and we briefly conversed until she left. I called my favorite cousin to tell her about the beautiful celebration and we talked about the goodness of God. She said, "I attend church more regularly now and God is changing my old thought patterns and ways." I encouraged her and said, "God faithfully forgives our sins, and we have to let some things go, before we receive the glory." She informed me of her recent baptism in the name of The Father, The Son, and The Holy Spirit. I congratulated her and shared my older brothers' planned baptism in the near future. We praised God for what He has done and what He is about to do for our family. We rejoiced in the Lord.

I went to bed and coughed, spat, coughed and spat like Papa. I couldn't sleep and got out of bed to read my Bible. I prayed and prayed in the Holy Ghost and called on Jesus. The Spirit of God led me to Bruce Wilkerson's "Secrets of the Vine." I skimmed the pages and stopped on the reference of Jesus, the vine and His Father, the vinedresser. The Spirit revealed that I have been the keeper of secrets. A few days prior, I asked the Lord, "Am I the keeper of my sister's secrets? As a confidant, I kept their secrets. While I was in the fire, their secrets ignited the flames because my ability to employ weapons of warfare was impaired. Particularly, several sisters revealed their secrets to me and said, "You're the only person I have told."

At an early age, I knew not to keep secrets. I 'memba when we slept three to four in a bed. I was about four years old, we lived in Lorain and I slept with one of my older sisters. One night, I peed in the bed, woke up early, changed my underwear, went to my parent's bedroom and told Mama a story. I told her to keep what I was about to tell her a secret which was my first mistake. I told Mama my sister wet the bed and peed on my underwear. I told her that I forgave my sister and volunteered to change the bed. Mama looked me straight in my face and said, "Don't lie on yo' sister, get yo' little butt in there and take a bath." Death and life are in the power of the tongue and Mama's anger spoke to me. After that, I learned how to hold my water. I don't think I ever peed the bed again. Sometimes in order to heal from something, you have to confront it.

While we're on the subject of pee and kinfolk, can we "talk story"? *I 'memba dem' cousins who peed in the bed every night. They peed well into their teenage years. One day, I walked into one of their bedrooms and almost puked. I asked my cousin what her issue was and she said, "While I'm asleep, I dream I'm on the toilet and pee on myself." I shook my head back and forth and tried to help her think of a more pleasant dream.*

As I continued to read "Secrets of the Vine", I envisioned **Jesus** as He walked through the Garden of Gethsemane and talked to His disciples. **The Spirit of God** ordered my steps and my eyes stayed planted on **the Word** garden. During that moment, **God** reminded me of my desire to garden and the desires of my heart that the devil tried to steal from me.

HE WHO HAS EARS LET HIM HEAR:
God's perfect will and order will be evident in the future Kingdom. The land of milk and honey is flowing in **God**'s goodness. Celebrate this day our daily bread (**The Word of God**). Enter His presence with thanksgiving in your hearts. He prepared the table in the presence of our enemies. Serve one another with gladness. As Christians, we have a right to eat from the tree of life. In the paradise of **God**, we will all rejoice and everything will be in perfect order. Be thankful for the gift of **God**. Dance like David danced in the presence of **the King**. Remember, secrets can over-burden you and **God** judges secrets through **Jesus Christ**.

Chapter 15

THE POWER OF PRAYER

COMING OUT OF THE FIRE: Thursday, February 15, 2007

SCRIPTURE FOR THE DAY: If my people, who are called by my name, will humble themselves and pray and seek my face and turn from their wicked ways, then will I hear from heaven and will forgive their sin and will heal their land. Now my eyes will be open and my ears attentive to the prayers offered in this place. 2 Chronicles 7:14 -15 (NIV)

I got up, made the bed, took my shower and got dressed for work. My husband prayed, kissed me and left. As soon as he left, a spirit of heaviness and uneasiness came upon me. I'm no stranger to spiritual warfare, but this particular warfare was like nothing I've ever experienced. The heaviness felt like I was on the verge of death. It felt like something or someone was about to be destroyed. The devil knew the "7" days of testing my faith were almost over and perseverance was at my door. I called on **Jesus** and some of my sisters and brothers-in-**Christ** to pray and fast with me until the midnight hour. I described to them my spiritual warfare and told them I needed to be covered. **The Spirit of**

God revealed, "Today is a day of significance, a day that would be etched in minds forever." In all things, God works for the good.

I reflected on the goodness of God and was determined to pray my way through. I put on the full armor of God, grabbed my weapon of warfare, The Bible and drove to church on base to pray. A minister met me at the church and we asked for a special room, she led us to the big room on the right and asked, "Is this room sufficient?" I answered, "No, it's too small" and requested the balcony. We went to the balcony and prayed in the Spirit. The Spirit of the Lord revealed through the minister, the Word, "Mirror." My life flashed before me and I reflected on the times when I was closest to God. The devil didn't want me to recall those times, nor did he want me to come out of the fire unscathed. For several hours, I cried to the Lord in the name of Jesus.

Before I left the church, I asked God to send Christians to my office to strengthen me. We have not, because we ask not. I arrived at work and my supervisor, the Captain said, "Chief, I thought you were out sick today." I replied, "I'm not sick." He looked at me and said, "You look sick." I told him I was at church all morning praying, he asked if we could talk and I said, "Sure." I asked him if he would mind if I talked candidly about spiritual wellness. He said, "Sure, Chief."

We talked about several weeks ago when I mentioned I was on my way to Bible study and what his reply was. He had replied, "I haven't been to church lately, but I need to go." I encouraged him and reminded him that the Bible says that we should not forsake the assembling of ourselves together. I said, "Sir, I don't know if you're aware, but I'm very strong in my faith and being a Christian means everything to me." He replied, "Chief, your faith is no secret to me or anyone else around you. Everyone knows how much you love **God** and how much your faith means to you." I smiled and apologized for my lack of availability due to my wilderness experience. He said, "Not a problem Chief, I appreciate **the Way** you carried the load last summer while I was deployed." He replied, "Concentrate on getting better and make it your number one priority." I replied, "Thank You."

I thanked **God** for a good Captain and went back to my office. Around noon, my pregnant coworker came in my office and we shared "The Good News." She confessed that **God** often speaks to her and she's reluctant to respond. I explained why it's important to obey **God** when He speaks and obedience is better than sacrifice. She agreed and professed that from this day forth, she'd act when **God** said act. She asked, "Did you see on television The Coming of **the Messiah** and the people with 666 tattooed to their bodies? It was on the television at the dining facility." I replied, "No" and researched the information online, but to no avail. I contacted the dining facility several times to find out what channel the television was on, but never got an answer or voice message. When I finally got through a messenger of Satan answered in a voice that sounded like a recording and said, "The enemy." I hung up the phone and said the devil is a liar. The devil tried to torment my mind, but I didn't belong to him. As a Christian, I knew to fight on. I emailed my church body and requested prayer and intercession.

*I 'memba when some of my aunts used to say they heard voices. The voice of the enemy, Satan, tormented several of them for years. They often confused the voice of Satan with the voice of **God**. Satan often told one of my aunts to do bad things and sometimes she responded to his voice through her actions. Thank **God**, she never hurt anyone. I 'memba when she chased me and my "bad cousins" with a butcher knife and accused us of stealing from her. She accused us of telling lies on her and accused my grandmother of stealing her boyfriend. One* *of my cousins ran to my grandmother's house and told her the voices were tormenting auntie and Mommy came with her weapon in hand (the Bible). Her spiritual gift of discerning spirits prompted her to tell everyone present to keep saying, "Jesus" and Mommy rebuked the evil spirit that tormented my aunt. Mommy said that my aunt knew of Jesus, but she didn't have a personal relationship with Him. The devil became a stronghold and she couldn't distinguish between the gentle voice of God and the voice of Satan. Mommy said she needed Jesus and deliverance.*

Another coworker came by my office and said, "Chief, I plan to take you up on your invitation to attend church soon." She said that her husband had no desire to attend, but knew she needed God. I explained how important it was for her to attend and told her God will change his heart based on her obedience. She agreed, hugged me and left the office.

I stayed close to my office all day, situations arose that tried to shake my faith and cloud my judgment. I was overwhelmed with suspenses and deadlines, but managed to resolve issues in record time. Near the end of the duty day, a coworker came by my office and said, "Chief, I've never seen you like this before. You've put out fires all day; it's as if you have a fire hose in your hands to water issues down." He had no idea that I had been in the fire for "7" days straight and today I extinguished the devils flames with my shield of faith and was on my way out of the fire.

I had no idea why the Lord had sent me to Florida after He stationed me in Colorado for only eight months. One of the Master Sergeants I worked with had told me on several occasions, "Chief, God sent you here to stop the bleeding." *Like the woman with an issue of blood, my nose bled almost everyday for about a year when I was about five years old. Sometimes, I thought it would never stop, but Mama said God would stop it. The only thing that soothed me was when I lifted my head toward God. Since Mama said God would stop it, I prayed that He would. Sometimes, I kept my head lifted and prayed for what seemed like hours before the bleeding stopped. Eventually I grew out of it.* Occasionally, my sons have nosebleeds and I remind them that when I was a child I had the same issue, but look at me now, God stopped the bleeding.

Toward the end of the duty day, my sister-in-Christ stopped by my office unannounced. Her presence comforted me and we "talked story." All day and into the night the devil tormented my mind. Close to midnight, I called on the elder of my church. I called Mama and asked her to pray for me and to call on my family to pray, too. At first, Mama hesitated, but The Spirit of the Lord reminded her of the generational anointing that flowed through Mommy and whose seed she was. I said, "Mama, I Am your seed and the devil is trying to destroy me." Then I said, "I'm Helen, Mama, have you ever known me not to be of sound mind, if my own Mama won't pray for me, then who will?" She replied, "You're absolutely right, I'll pray and call the family to pray, too." The elder and Minister King came by my house to pray for me. My Angel and a witness came, too. Before the clock struck midnight, for the first time my family prayed together on one accord in the name of Jesus. Not only did my family and the church pray, but my sisters-in-Christ and some of their family members prayed, too. We prayed and God got the glory. The devil wanted to destroy me, but God had other plans. Perseverance had finished its work and I was on my way to maturity and completion. I lacked nothing and slept for the first time in "7" days.

HE WHO HAS EARS LET HIM HEAR:
In these last days, spiritual warfare is on the rise. Satan torments us in different ways. The sheep know the voice of the true Shepherd, the Messiah. Satan is the enemy, the accuser, the adversary, and the author of confusion. He comes to steal, kill, and destroy. When the enemy torments you, call Jesus and the

saints for prayer and intercession. Resist the devil and he will flee. Thank God for His grace and mercy and for spiritual weapons. Put on your full armor of God and stay equipped for battle. The power of prayer and faith moves mountains. Humble yourself and pray. Lift your head to the hills from whence cometh your help. The blood of **Jesus** covers us; He is our **Intercessor**. God allows us to go through fires so that He can reveal His power and revelation knowledge. Satan is working overtime; he knows his time on earth is short. God is pouring out His **Spirit** and equipping us for victory.

Chapter 16

SALVATION

For **Jesus** is the one referred to in the Scriptures, where it says, "He is the stone you builders rejected, which has become the capstone. Salvation is found in no one else, for there is no other name under heaven given to men by which we must be saved." Acts 4:11-12 (NIV)

He, who has ears, let him hear. The Bible says in Romans 3:23 (KJV) that all have sinned, and come short of the glory of **God**. We were born into the sinful nature. **God** desires to save us through salvation. Salvation offers us freedom and is deliverance from evil, danger, or trouble. It is the gift of **God** through **Christ** to save souls. It's an opportunity to be free from the powers of sin, free from hell, free from bondage and free from condemnation.

By grace and through faith, I received salvation on November 3, 1991, while stationed in Las Vegas. I was baptized in the name of *The Father, The Son,* and *The Holy Spirit* in 1993 while attending Calvary Revival Church in Norfolk, VA. A **Teacher** in accordance with the five-fold ministry in Ephesians 4:11 (NIV) prayed the prayer of salvation with me and my sister-in-**Christ**, Bridget Howard.

Our prayer of salvation was similar to this:

"**Lord Jesus**, I ask You to come into my heart and transform me by the renewing of my mind, body, and **Spirit**. I repent from sin and ask You to cleanse me and make me a new creature. I believe in my heart and confess with my mouth that **Jesus Christ** is **Lord**. I believe that You were born of a Virgin Mary and that You died on Calvary so that we would have life and have it more abundantly. I believe that You rose on the third day with all power in Your hand. **Lord** forgive me of my sins. You are KING OF KINGS AND LORD OF LORDS."

After we received salvation, our Teacher prophesied over both of us. She said that the Angels in heaven were rejoicing because both of us committed our lives to **Jesus** and that **God** was going to use both of us in a mighty way. The blood of **Jesus** saves and He alone is the **Savior**. There is power in the name, **Jesus**. He has given each of us a perfect will to choose. You can choose to be in perfect peace in the **Lord** or to continue in the ways of this world. The Bible says in Isaiah 55:8 (NIV), "For my thoughts are not your thoughts, neither are your ways my ways, declares the **Lord**." **God** desires to make His mysteries known unto those who truly love Him and desire to serve Him.

God wants to heal and restore you. Restoration may come after you look in the mirror, remove the veil and uncover yourself. Let **God** take you through the temporal fire (a period of refinement). While in the fire, you may feel like you're in the wilderness, just hold on, **God** isn't through with you yet. The fire reminds you of where you've been (your past), where you are (your present/gift), and most importantly, where you're going (your future). Count it all joy when the fire intensifies daily and exposes **the Root** of issues. This exposure may cause you great pain and suffering, sometimes sickness, disease and maybe sleepless nights.

When you can't sleep, read the Bible and rest in the shadow of **The Almighty**. **The Holy Spirit** reveals sins in the fire, the times you lied, stole, cheated and so on and so forth. You grow in the fire, but you also reap what you have sown. The harvest is plentiful but the laborers are few (Matthew 9:37, ESV). Let go and let **God** unravel you so that you can get your breakthrough. He doesn't put more on you than you can bear. Fires regenerate (birth), remove (death), and restore (resurrect) in order for **God** to reveal His glory and make His mysteries known. To **God** be the glory for all the things that He hath done.

He hath done a great work in us. It's harvest time, time to be set free from the entrapments of this world. He loves you more than you could ever love yourself. The peace of **God** surpasses all understanding. **God** wants your soul to be at peace because He is the **Prince of Peace**. He knew you before He formed you in your mother's womb and He made you in His image. You are **God**'s incorruptible seed. Let His peace flow through you like a river. When the storms rage in your life, He will shelter you and calm the waters. He will renew your mind, body and soul in **Christ Jesus**. He has kept you here for such a time as this. You are the blessing of Abraham, a chosen generation, a child of **the Most High God**, an heir of the Kingdom. Look in the mirror and see that you are blessed.

You're blessed and highly favored in the **Lord**. Reflect back over your life and rejoice in the times **God** charged His Angels over you to protect you. Let go of the past, **God** will never remind you of your past. His desire is for you to move forward and walk in the light. You are a living testimony of **God**'s grace and mercy. **God** didn't protect you in the midst of the storm and bring you out of the fire for you to keep it a secret. He delivered you from the hand of the enemy so that you could spread "The Good News." Go and "talk-story" about what He has done for you. Heal someone else's land. When we cause others to error from their ways, it covers multitudes of sin.

Guard your heart and mind from the sinful nature of this earthly realm. Position yourself to seek His face and to hear from Him. Seek peace (tranquil state of rest, reflection, and restoration) where you fellowship with God. Peace is your secret place (shelter) and it will make you steadfast and immoveable. Peace will make you be still. When you know that your sins are forgiven, you find peace in rest and rest in peace.

Keep your countenance at all times and let your light continue to shine even during the darkest times of your life, trust in the Lord to make a way in the valley and wilderness experiences. The Lord is my light and my salvation whom shall I fear (Psalm 27:1, ESV)? Call on Jesus anytime and praise Him in spite of your experiences. The favor of God will rest over you and He will provide a ram in the bush to remove your thorns. Place your feet on the Rock of His salvation. He desires to meet you at the river to baptize you in the name of The Father, The Son, and The Holy Spirit. He will deliver you from the hands of the enemy.

When the enemy (accusers, liars, snakes, loud voices, etc) tempts you and tries to steal, kill, and destroy, God will judge them through Christ Jesus. Christ overcame temptation. Acts of the sinful nature rob you of your inheritance. Keep your faith and stand. Rebuke the devil in the name of Jesus and take back everything he stole from you. The devil is the source of your woes. Perseverance in the fire refines you, but God promised to never leave you, nor forsake you. He desires to set the captives free. Obey his commands; obedience is better than sacrifice.

The Word of God is always in season. His unchanging hand is the same yesterday, today and forever. Jesus prepared the table and God gave us this day our daily bread (provision), rejoice and be exceedingly glad in it. Take advantage of every opportunity set before you. Praise Him in the storm, praise Him in the good times and praise Him always. Clothe yourself in humility and put on the full armor of God. Jesus won the battle and paid the price in full. Take up your cross, confess your sins, forgive, forget and follow God so that He may increase your territory and add purpose to your life. Christ came so that we may have life and have it more abundantly. If you trust God, He will break the chains and deliver families from generational curses. Your seed shall be blessed.

Let's "talk story" about how blessed we are. Let's pray together and make time for family. Teach the children about Jesus, to honor and obey their parents and to respect elders. They don't need the Game Boys, PSPs, Play stations, Xboxes, and televisions in their rooms as much as they need to know about Jesus. Information technology put us on the wrong track. Children need boundaries and to know that parents make mistakes, too. As parents we need to say, "I'm sorry for the things I did wrong, but Lord knows I did the best I could with what I had and sometimes it wasn't enough." The devil wants us to leave this world bitter and resentful, but God desires for us to love each other and to be happy on earth, as it is in heaven.

Love one another; this is a commandment from God. Love your enemies as yourself. Apologize to one another today, mend the brokenness and heal one another's souls. We need one another in these last days. Concentrate on the legacy you plan to leave for future generations. Your house may not have felt like a home, but the home you despise, may be the one you reproduce. Tend to the sick and shut in. When your burdens are heavy, call the saints for prayer. Pray for those in prison and encourage them to keep the faith. Forgive our trespasses and those who have trespassed against us. We need to heal today, not tomorrow. Reunite and vow to be there for one another in good times and bad. We are family.

Lord, please remove the scales from our eyes and strengthen our minds, bodies and souls. Rebuke the demonic spirits and deliver us from the hand of the enemy. **Holy Spirit**, grant us peace that surpasses all understanding. Restore in us a clean heart and right spirit. The hands of **Jesus** are healing hands. **God** said, "It is finished." His invitation still stands.

My soul finds rest in **God** alone; my salvation comes from Him.
Psalm 62:1 (NIV)

HE WHO HAS EARS LET HIM HEAR:
Jesus saves.

Chapter 17

MY REVELATION

Now, brothers, if I come to you and speak in tongues, what good will I be to you, unless I bring you some revelation or knowledge or prophecy or word of instruction? 1 Corinthians 14:6 (NIV)

I thought I was finished with this book, but **the Holy Spirit** revealed He had more to say. Revelation is the last chapter of the Bible, His Book and "My Revelation" is the finale to this book. To God be the glory for all the things He hath done. On August 22, 2007, Mother Helen's house went up in flames and in the natural, my Uncle Nathan Nelson's earthly body perished in the fire. John 3:16 (NIV) says, "For God so loved the world that He gave his **One and Only Son** that whoever believes in Him shall not perish but have eternal life." Uncle Nathan was a Preacher; therefore, I rejoice because I'll see him again on Judgment Day.

Can we "talk story"? While stationed in Virginia around 1997-98, I watched a movie called "Down in the Delta" directed by Maya Angelou. The movie spoke life to me. It signified the importance of family history and the need to "talk story" from one generation to another. In the movie, a silver candelabrum, named Nathan was the family heirloom (conversation piece) that ignited the "talk story" flames. The candelabrum initially belonged to a slave owner who had exchanged a slave named Nathan for it. Nathan's son Jesse witnessed the slave auction and one day Jesse stole the candelabrum off the master's fireplace mantel. Nathan's legacy was passed on from generation to generation. One generation shall praise Your works to another, and shall declare Your mighty acts (Psalm 145:4, NIV).

My heart's desire is to finish a project I started on my family genealogy. Approximately two weeks before I attended the 2007 Nelson Family Reunion, my brother-in-Christ who has the spiritual gift of prophecy, revealed that one of my uncles at the reunion had some information to share with me. He said the information would connect some of the pieces of my story (life).

I went to the reunion inspired with expectation of a blessing. The night before our return trip home, I had some unfinished business to finish. My Uncle Israel Daughtery invited my sons and me to his house. My girlfriend drove to see me from McConnell Air Force Base and we decided to go by my uncles for a visit. Upon arriving, he shared some information with us about the Battle of Armageddon, as well as some significant numbers in the Book of Revelation. Although I was grateful, his information didn't connect any pieces so we returned to the hotel and my girlfriend departed. My sons and I continued on our journey to Mother Helen's house. Uncle Nathan inherited the house after my grandmother died in 1995. When I arrived, the house appeared smaller, the sidewalk was shorter and the porch wasn't nearly as high as I remembered it.

When we entered, the front loaded wood stove with the chimney connector still extended through the ceiling in the living room. Uncle Nathan had taken care of Mother Helen's home, adding and preserving it with respect. Although Mother Helen was with the Lord, you could feel her presence in the house. Newspaper clippings and scrapbook items were scattered throughout the front rooms. I explained to Uncle Nathan my desire to complete the family genealogy and asked if he had anything of significance that belonged to Mother Helen that he could share with me. He explained that after Mother Helen died family members came by the house and took most of her possessions. He said, "I do have something for you."

Uncle Nathan went into the dining room, sifted through the clutter and retrieved two scrapbooks that belonged to Mother Helen. He passed them to me and I sensed they were the missing pieces of my story. As I carefully opened the cover, inscribed on the first page was: "Mrs. Helen Nelson's scrapbook, bought August 1963." Contained within the first pages was the original newspaper clipping of my great grandmother, Emma Reid's obituary. On the same page was the last letter Mother Helen received from her mother before her mother's death on June 22, 1963. The letter was is in its original envelope with a five-cent stamp on it, dated April 19, 1963. It was obvious that Mother Helen's seed of excellence was her mother's legacy to her. I discovered my roots through my great grandmother Emma Reid, born in 1885 to my great-great grandparents Minerva Strickland (a slave) and George Alexander. I sat there in Mother Helen's living room like a little girl in Mother Helen's garden. I envisioned myself lying in her bed and waking up to her sweet voice as it whispered, "Rise and shine, Sunshine."

Uncle Nathan shared intimate details of his life with me. He said his inability to speak eloquently often caused people to overlook his instruction. The Bible says in 1 Corinthians 12:22 (NIV), "On the contrary, those parts of the body that seem to be weaker are indispensable, and the parts that we think are less honorable we treat with special honor." We are all members of one body, the body of Christ and Uncle Nathan's words were revelation knowledge to my ears. The power of his tongue spoke life into me and I took extensive notes about our family. We talked story about the goodness of God. One thing he shared was his God-given spiritual gift of the word of wisdom concerning death. He said God forewarned him of the death of Daddy Nelson and Uncle Vernon. He said it was as if God was preparing him to handle death. I revealed to him how God birthed this book and when I mentioned, "The name of the book is *7 Days in the Fire*," tears began to stream down his face almost like streams of living water. I didn't feel a need to question his tears because it appeared he was crying unto the Lord. They appeared to be tears of joy, not pain.

When I left Uncle Nathan, words could not describe the treasure in my possession. I took several pictures of the house before I departed and as I walked toward the car the Holy Spirit had me take one last glance of the house and He said, "Restore the House." It was an awkward feeling because at the time I didn't fully understand the significance of "Restore the House." I could hardly wait to get back to the hotel room and read the letters written by my great grandmother. In one of the letters, she thanked Mother Helen for sending her two dollars. In another, she mentioned ironing all of her clothes one day; in another letter, she mentioned her garden. All the letters are in their original envelopes. I have "7" letters from my great grandmother, the oldest letter is sixty-four years old (dated Apr 26, 1943) and has a three-cent stamp on it. I also have a letter from Uncle Nathan to Mother Helen, which he wrote while he was in the Army dated July 6, 1960. The scrapbook contains a postcard from Mother Helen's baby sister (my great Aunt) Mildred Reid dated May 18, 1942, and it has a one-cent stamp on it. All the treasures date before I was born on November 24, 1964.

When I returned to Florida, I couldn't wait to share "The Good News" about the treasure in my possession with my favorite cousin and other family members. I praised God and rejoiced in the fact that God and my Uncle Nathan entrusted me with the scrapbooks. I mentioned to my niece that I desired to restore Mother Helen's house if the opportunity ever presented itself. In addition, I said, "If Mother Helen's house ever caught on fire, it would go up in flames because of all the newspapers 'historical documents' inside. "

After meeting with Uncle Nathan, I would occasionally ask **the Lord** if I needed to return Mother Helen's scrapbooks to him. On August 22, 2007 at approximately 3:00 a.m., Mother Helen's house caught on fire. I received a call from my cousin around 9:00 a.m., stating that Uncle Nathan died in the fire. **The Holy Spirit** had me look up the name Nathan and it means "Giver" in Hebrew. The newspaper clipping of Uncle Nathan's death revealed that when firefighters arrived on the scene and broke the door down they faced intense heat and flames. Firefighters said they found him in the bathroom of the house. The bars on the windows and the back door were barricaded shut, which more than likely caused him not to be able to escape. One news station reported the flames were seen several miles away.

Uncle Nathan's funeral was on Tuesday, August 28, 2007. I couldn't attend, but my Daddy, sister and brother attended. My sister went by Mother Helen's house and said, "Most of the front burned to the ground, but there was a gold curtain that hung in his bedroom window." Uncle Nathan had an open-casket funeral and several hairs on his head were singed. The program described him as an active member of his church who loved to sing. He enjoyed visiting elderly people and was always the first in line to help people. **Lord** knows we will miss you Uncle Nathan. I desire to sit on Mother Helen's couch with him again to "talk story."

Uncle Nathan ignited a fire in me that will burn forever. He preserved the family legacy and gave me a double portion of the inheritance. Like Shadrach, Meshach, and Abednego in the Book of Daniel, I have been through the fire of judgment. My soul is at rest because I came out as pure gold. Matthew 3:12 (NIV) says, "His winnowing fork is in his hand, and he will clear his threshing floor, gathering his wheat into the barn and burning up the chaff with unquenchable fire." The fire represents a shedding of old things and with every trial and fire there is revelation. God is finishing and completing what he started in 2007. In 2008, God will usher in new beginnings. Get your house in order. Hold on my brothers and sisters, it's gonna' be all right. Revelation knowledge from God is powerful.

In the Book of Revelation, the Lord speaks of victory to the "seven churches." The Bible says, "God's children are the church." The church is the temple of God. HE WHO HAS AN EAR, LET HIM HEAR WHAT THE SPIRIT SAYS TO THE CHURCHES:

- ✦ To him who overcomes, I will give the right to the tree of life, which is in the paradise of God (Rev 2:7, NIV)
- ✦ He who overcomes will not be hurt at all by the second death (Rev 2:11, NIV)
- ✦ To him who overcomes, I will give some of the hidden manna. I will also give him a white stone with a new name on it, known only to him who receives it (Rev 2:17, NIV)
- ✦ To him who overcomes and does my will to the end, I will give authority over the nations (Rev 2:26, NIV)
- ✦ He who overcomes will, like them, be dressed in white. I will never blot out his name from the book of life, but will acknowledge his name before my Father and his angels (Rev 3:5, NIV)
- ✦ Him who overcomes I will make a pillar in the temple of my God. Never again will he leave it. I will write on him the name of my God and the name of the city of my God, the new Jerusalem, which is coming down out of heaven from my God; and I will also write on him my new name (Rev 3:11-12, NIV)

+ To him who overcomes, I will give the right to sit with me on my throne, just as I overcame and sat down with my **Father** on his throne (Rev 3:21, NIV)

For our **God** is a consuming fire. (Hebrews 12:29, NIV)

THE INTERPRETATION
OF THE VISION/MESSAGE
OF THE BOOK

I was unable to sleep from February 8-14, 2007. I was in the fire for "7" days straight, resting in the shadow of **the Almighty**. On February 15, I experienced a spiritual warfare like never before, the devil tried to destroy me. On February 16, after a peaceful night of sleep, God used my long piano fingers to type *7 Days in the Fire*. God sheltered me from the hand of the enemy and I came out of the fire unscathed, as pure gold. I thank Him for His grace and mercy.

God gave me the vision of this book and I understand it from a personal account, but the "Healing and Restoration" message is universal. The universal message of this book is "Heal the body/ church and restore the house before the fire." Read Ephesians, Chapter 4 (NIV):

Unity in the Body of Christ
"As a prisoner for the **Lord**, then, I urge you to live a life worthy of the calling you have received. Be completely humble and gentle; be patient, bearing with one another in love. Make every effort to keep the unity of **the Spirit** through the bond of peace. There is one body and one **Spirit**—just as you were called to one hope when you were called— one **Lord**, one faith, one baptism; one **God** and **Father** of all, who is over all and through all and in all. But to each one of us grace has been given as **Christ** apportioned it. This is why it says: "When he ascended on high, he led captives in his train and gave gifts to men." (What does "he ascended" mean except that he also descended to the lower, earthly

regions? He who descended is the very one who ascended higher than all the heavens, in order to fill the whole universe.) It was he who gave some to be apostles, some to be prophets, some to be evangelists, and some to be pastors and teachers, to prepare God's people for works of service, so that the body of Christ may be built up until we all reach unity in the faith and in the knowledge of the Son of God and become mature, attaining to the whole measure of the fullness of Christ. Then we will no longer be infants, tossed back and forth by the waves, and blown here and there by every wind of teaching and by the cunning and craftiness of men in their deceitful scheming. Instead, speaking the truth in love, we will in all things grow up into him who is the Head, that is, Christ. From him the whole body, joined and held together by every supporting ligament, grows and builds itself up in love, as each part does its work.

Living as Children of Light

So I tell you this, and insist on it in the Lord, that you must no longer live as the Gentiles do, in the futility of their thinking. They are darkened in their understanding and separated from the life of God because of the ignorance that is in them due to the hardening of their hearts. Having lost all sensitivity, they have given themselves over to sensuality so as to indulge in every kind of impurity, with a continual lust for more. You, however, did not come to know Christ that way. Surely you heard of him and were taught in him in accordance with the truth that is in Jesus. You were taught, with regard to your former way of life, to put off your old self, which is being corrupted by its deceitful desires; to be made new in the attitude of your minds; and to put on the new self, created to be like God in true righteousness and holiness. Therefore each of you must put off falsehood and speak truthfully to his neighbor, for we are all members of one body. "In your anger do not sin": Do not let the sun go down while you are still angry, and do not give the devil a foothold. He who has been stealing must steal no longer, but must work, doing something useful with his own hands, that he may have something to share with those in need. Do not let any unwholesome talk come out of your mouths, but only what is helpful for building others up according to their needs, that it may benefit those who listen. And do not grieve **the Holy Spirit** of **God**, with whom you were sealed for the day of redemption. Get rid of all bitterness, rage and anger, brawling and slander, along with every form of malice. Be kind and compassionate to one another, forgiving each other, just as **Christ God** forgave you."

The bride speaks of the New Jerusalem in Revelation 21:1-9 (NIV), "Then I saw a new heaven and a new earth, for the first heaven and the first earth had passed away, and there was no longer any sea. I saw the Holy City, the new Jerusalem, coming down out of heaven from **God**, prepared as a bride beautifully dressed for her husband. And I heard a loud voice from the throne saying, "Now the dwelling of **God** is with men, and he will live with them. They will be his people, and **God** himself will be with them and be their **God**. He will wipe every tear from their eyes. There will be no more death or mourning or crying or pain, for the old order of things has passed away. He who was seated on the throne said, "I am making everything new!" Then he said, "Write this down, for these words are trustworthy and true." He said to me: "It is done. **I am the Alpha and the Omega, the Beginning and the End.** To him who is thirsty I will give to drink without cost from the spring of the water of life. He who overcomes will inherit all this, and I will be his **God** and he will be my son. But the cowardly, the unbelieving, the vile, the murderers, the sexually immoral, those who practice magic arts, the idolaters and all liars – their place will be in the fiery lake of burning sulfur. This is the second death." One of the seven angels who had the seven bowls full of the seven last plagues came and said to me, "Come, I will show you the bride, the wife of **the Lamb**."

God has a divine plan and order for His children. The family unit is in need of healing and restoration. He wants us to claim our inheritance and to take back everything the devil stole from us. If we are too busy to seek Him, we will not recognize His voice when He calls us. God desires for us to spend more time with him. The Bible says in Proverbs 6:33 (NIV), "But seek first his kingdom and his righteousness, and all these things will be given to you as well."

As I typed this book, **the Holy Spirit** continually spoke "Bible" to me. From Genesis (the beginning) to Revelation (the end) when you look in the mirror you will see yourself in His book (the Bible). **The Beginning and the End** is in God's hands. I pray that this book will bring you out of the fire and you will have a stronger desire to listen and obey the voice of God. Study to show thyself approved unto God, a workman that needeth not be ashamed, rightly dividing **the Word** of truth according to 2 Timothy 2:15 (KJV).

Lord, Jesus at the right hand of **the Father,** speak to us. Sit Your children at Your feet and "talk story" to us. At night, lay our heads on Your pillow and give us rest. We desire to be more like You. Cover us in Your righteousness and teach us Your ways. Your grace and mercy brought us through; restore in us a clean heart and right spirit. He maketh me to lie down in green pastures—that's REST. Thank You, **Holy Spirit.**

Everything You revealed to me in February, You have brought full circle to complete this book. This book consumed me for ten months, but I was determined to finish what You started. As I labored in reverence and awe seeking clarification to the visions You revealed, You answered "Yes", and **"Amen"** according to Your promise. **Holy Spirit,** You sent Your mighty Angels to be encamped around me and I will always lift up the name of **Jesus.**

What a mighty **God** we serve. Thank You for Your dispensation of grace. It is finished. You are the **Author and Finisher of our Faith**.

SONGS OF DELIVERANCE

The following artists/songs covered me as I typed the *7 Days in the Fire* chapters. God used these Angels and their song titles to strengthen and cover me.

Dakota Smith, "The things we do for Love"
Dottie Peoples, "Inseparable"
Euclid Gray, "Are you a letter"
Diann McMillian, "God is"
The Preachers Kid, "A Better Man"
Shekinah Glory, "Yes"
Valerie Boyd, "Victory"
PAJAM, "Father", "Sing"
Spensha Baker, "Purpose"
Timothy Wright, "Jesus, Jesus, Jesus"
Sounds of Blackness, "Hold On"
Ruth Bradford, "So many times"
Candi Staton, "It's your season"
5 AM Praise, "I smile"
Hezekiah Walker, "99 ½"
The Florida Mass Choir, "I cannot tell it all"
Lucinda Moore, "Pressure into Praise"
Devoted, "Let's go back"
Lee Wms, "Next time around"
Rev Paul Jones, "I won't Complain"
Angela Spivey, "These thorns"
Dr Varnard Johnson, "Yes I'm a Believer"
Bishop Paul S. Morton, "True Praise"
Troy Sneed, "Hallelujah"

Dr Leonard Scott, "Come and go with me"
Lennie Battle, "Call Him anytime"
Brown Boys, "Hallelujah Slide"
Myrna Summers, "Uncloudy Day"
Dorothy Norwood, "Victory is Mine"
Donald Lawrence, "Finale"
Louise & Amp, "We aint what we were"
Mississippi Choir, "I'm not tired yet"
Virtue, "Follow Me"
The McClurkin Project, "We Praise You"
Neal Robinson, "It's on the way"
Prodigal 1, "It's Time"
Wilmington Mass Choir, "Take it Away"
MFMP, "This is the day of the Harvest"
Kenneth Wilson, "Go and sin no more"
Bishop David Evans, "Let it be me"
Deitrick Haddon, "Heaven Knows"
Colorado Mass, "Praise till you break through"
7 Sons of Soul, "Praying for you"
Brent Jones & the T.B. Mobb, "Good Times"
Moses Tyson Junior, "I'll take you there"
Adriane Archie, "Welcome", "It is well"
Marvin Sapp, "Not now doesn't mean never"
Fred Hammond, "No Greater love"
Dorothy Norwood, "Victory today is mine"
Doug & Melvin Waters, "Soothing Water"
Israel & New Breed, "Turn it around"
Rev James Cleveland, "What should I do?"
BeBe & CeCe Winans, "I'll take you there"
Tremaine Hawkins, "Excellent **Lord**"
Shirley Murdock, "I love me better than that"
Worship the House, "**Jehovah Jireh**"
Vanessa Bell Armstrong, "So good to me"
Larry Trotter, "The **Lord** is Blessing Me"
Melvin Williams, "Pray on my child"

Kenny Lewis and the One Voice, "Everybody Everybody"
Bishop Ronald Brown, "Down by the River"
Clara Ward Singers, "Packing Up"
Yolanda Adams, "Step Aside"
Helen Baylor, "I'm lifting up the Name of Jesus"
Dorinda Clark, "Don't nobody know"
Praise II Choir, "As good as God has been to me"
Reeds Temple Choir, "Oh what He's done for me"
Canton Spirituals, "Singing in the Heavenly Choir"
Alvin Darling & Celebration, "From me to you"
Luther & Deborah Barnes, "I'm still holding you"
Billy Rivers, "Let's Celebrate/Worship Christ"
Bishop Leonard Scott, "Pentecostal Praise Medley"
Beau Williams, "Work me till I sweat", "Wonderful"
Gospel Music Workshop of America, "Anticipation"
New Jersey Mass Choir, "Fight on Christian, Fight on"
Apostle Donald Alford & the Gathering, "It's all about you"
T.D Jakes and D. Lawrence, "The Lady, Her Lover & Lord"
Rev Robert Lowe & Generations, "I won't let go till you Bless Me"
Fread Battle & the Temple Worshippers,
    "If I had 10 thousand tongues"
Kirk Franklin,
    "What ya' looking for", "Look at me now", "Looking for you"
Chicago Mass Choir, "Whatever you want God's got it",
    "Nobody like Jesus", "I'm going with Jesus", "I pray we'll
    all be ready"

HE WHO HAS EARS
LET HIM HEAR

Chapter 1: My Genesis
HE WHO HAS EARS LET HIM HEAR:

Refer to the Bible, the Book of Genesis to gain a better understanding of your "Roots" and genealogy. You were created in the image of God. As children of God, we are Abraham's seed, heirs of the Kingdom according to the promise. We come from a proud heritage. Jesus is the Root, the foundation. There is power in the name, Jesus and He is the Light of the World. Somebody prayed for you and is praying for you. Don't be discouraged by what you didn't have, praise God for what you have. Seek God for wisdom and instruction and lean not on your own understanding. God kept you alive to fulfill your purpose.

Chapter 2: Rest
HE WHO HAS EARS LET HIM HEAR:

We all get weary, but God will not put more on you than you can bear. When you're in a storm, seek God first and rest in the shadow of the Almighty. God has charged Angels to watch over you. Turn your pressure into praise. Get a song in your spirit and sing unto the Lord. Everyday is significant. Yesterday's trial may provide strength for today's wilderness experience. Let your light shine by doing unto others as you would have them do unto you. Keep your countenance at all times; the look on your face is your storyboard. Pray without ceasing and teach your children to pray.

Chapter 3: 'Memba When?
HE WHO HAS EARS LET HIM HEAR:

Our past shapes and molds our character. Build off the foundation of the past and consider it a stepping stone, not a stumbling block. God gave us our present day as a gift, rejoice and be glad in it. The blood of Jesus can heal your past. Run the race and persevere. Work toward your potential and press victoriously toward your mark. Remember to teach your seed about the value of a dollar. The love of money is the root of evil. Worship God, not money. Praise God we are not what we used to be.

Chapter 4: Faith of God
HE WHO HAS EARS LET HIM HEAR:

We are never alone. During sickness and disease, God will soothe your soul. Everyone goes through the furnace of afflictions. God does not take pleasure in our suffering. When your heart is troubled, keep the faith. Find comfort in the Bible. Trust and believe in the Word of God and lean not on your own understanding. The grace of God is sufficient in the fire. Jesus died on the cross and His blood covers us. He suffered for our transgressions. Exercise your faith and fear not.

Chapter 5: The Harvest
HE WHO HAS EARS LET HIM HEAR:

Respect elders. Train up children in the fear and admonition of the Lord. The harvest belongs to Christ, the firstfruit. There is an appropriate time and season for everything under the sun. God determines when we sow and when we reap. In between seasons, He prunes us in the form of trials and tribulations. The pruning stage shapes and molds our character; sometimes this stage is painful. Satan's weeds will tempt you because he desires to steal, kill, and destroy your seed. Temptations come in many forms, to include threats and promises. When the seed is nourished, it gives life and energy to the Root. The harvest speaks of healing and restoration, deliverance, completion and maturation. The harvest is worth the wait. God has given us the authority to trample over snakes and to overcome the power of the enemy. Don't be afraid to cast your net into the river. When storms come, continue to stand on "the Rock." His outstretched hand will deliver you from the hand of the enemy and make you "fishers of men." There is no condemnation for whatever secrets you have.

Chapter 6: The Children of God
HE WHO HAS EARS LET HIM HEAR:

My Papa died February "7", 1968 (my wilderness experience began almost forty years later on the night of February "7", 2007). Almost forty years ago, the late Dr. Martin Luther King said he saw the Promised Land in his last speech, "I see the Promised Land." The children of God have been in the wilderness for forty years, but 2007 is a year of completion. Get ready to cross over to new beginnings in 2008. His children are the chosen generation. God tells us if we are faithful over a few things that He will make us rulers over many. Children also need discipline and correction. Spare the rod and spoil the child. We are a royal priesthood. Forgive those who have hurt you. Seek God and reap His favor.

Chapter "7": Temptation
HE WHO HAS EARS LET HIM HEAR:

God has granted all of us a certain amount of grace, mercy, and peace but certain acts rob us of our inheritance. The devil comes like a thief in the night to steal our joy and he'll use anything or anyone to tempt us, even family members. The devil tempted Jesus; rest assured he also tempts us, just as Christ overcame temptation, so can we. Everything the devil means for bad, God can use it for good. God knows our hearts and He forgives us. There is no condemnation for those in Christ Jesus. Death and life are in the power of the tongue, but Jesus came so that we would have life and have it more abundantly. Somebody is praying for your deliverance from sin. Live according to the Fruits of the

Spirit (love, joy, peace, patience, kindness, goodness, faithfulness, gentleness, and self-control) not according to the sinful nature.

Chapter 8: Set the Captives Free
HE WHO HAS EARS LET HIM HEAR:

When we fail to seek God, we become prisoners enslaved in the sinful nature of this world. God desires to set the captives free from the bondages of sin through freedom in Christ. As Christians, we have to experience a new birth of the Spirit rather than the flesh. When we allow situations and circumstances to become strongholds in our lives we live in bondage. God will do whatever is necessary and go to great lengths to get our attention. Call on the name of Jesus when your pain seems too heavy to bear. He'll bring you through the fire. If you give up, you may stunt the growth of your seed or never give birth to the seed. Rebuke the devil and break the chains of bitterness, pride and envy. Although you are tempted or you may stray away from God, He is ever-present and His arms are always open wide to invite you into the Kingdom. Angels rejoice in homecomings. Dedicate or rededicate your life to Jesus and watch Him move mountains.

Chapter 9: The Reunion
HE WHO HAS EARS LET HIM HEAR:

Sudden death awakens you. It makes you think of the significance of each day. Life is not as predictable as we tend to believe. Death enlightens us of the realization of our vulnerabilities. We rationalize the good, the bad, and the ugly. Accept the fact that God is the only one in control at all times. Forgive and love one another in life because if you wait until death it is too late. Death is not only physical, but we must die daily to live a godly life. God is ever-present, we need to reunite and not allow the cares of this world to separate us from God or one another.

Chapter 10: The Favor of God
HE WHO HAS EARS LET HIM HEAR:

The favor of God is awesome. The Spirit dwells in us and intercedes for us when we call out to Him. The Holy Spirit rewards us with spiritual gifts and His favor is everlasting. Jesus desires to have a relationship with us. Get to know Him for yourself. When sickness and disease come against you, seek His face and pray for favor. God allows us to grow in favor with Him and with men. Is your name written in the book of Life? Do you know Jesus? Avail yourself of God and be purged of all that is not of Him. Purging is a form of deliverance. When you walk in the image of God, favor is more abundant.

Chapter 11: Obedience
HE WHO HAS EARS LET HIM HEAR:

You have not because you ask not. Make your requests known unto God and be specific. Obedience is better than sacrifice. When you pray, pray for God's perfect will to be done. When the Holy Spirit speaks, obey His commands. God rewards obedience and His promises are "Yes" and "Amen." As a child of God, you have authority and power through the Holy Spirit. Seek divine order and intervention at all times. God is pouring out His Spirit through His miracles, signs, and wonders. You can live in paradise on earth and in heaven. God is faithful.

Chapter 12: Sacrifice
HE WHO HAS EARS LET HIM HEAR:

Our children are a gift from God. Train up children in the way they should go, God will finish what you have started. In our weakness, the grace of God is sufficient. Praise Him while you're going through tribulations. We have to decrease for God to increase. Jesus was the sacrificial Lamb and He died so we would have life more abundantly. He paid the price in full once and for all. God gives us a perfect will to choose. Lay your burdens down and tend to the needs of others. It's not about you! Give God your best and share with others. Love God and reaffirm His greatness. Speak life.

Chapter 13: The devil is a Liar
HE WHO HAS EARS, LET HIM HEAR:

The devil is a liar. Uproot the root of issues; if you don't the issues will continue to grow. We all have seeds that need to be uprooted. The weeds (Satan) have choked us. The enemy can be so deeply rooted that it destroys "the inner me." Rebuke the devil when he says no one understands you better than him. God made you in His image and no one knows or understands you better than Him. The snares of the enemy are a form of bondage and entrapment. Sometimes healing comes from confrontation; past wounds need to be exposed. Exposure can lead to closure. Pride comes before the fall. If you desire wholeness, touch the hem of His garment. Jesus was wounded for our transgressions and pierced for our iniquities. He paid the price so you wouldn't have to. Be healed. Don't let the evil secrets that the devil planted to enslave you; seek to understand the secrets of the Kingdom of Heaven. With God, all things are possible.

Chapter 14: The Wedding Feast
HE WHO HAS EARS LET HIM HEAR:

God's perfect will and order will be evident in the future Kingdom. The land of milk and honey is flowing in God's goodness. Celebrate this day our daily bread (The Word of God). Enter His presence with thanksgiving in your hearts. He prepared the table in the presence of our enemies. Serve one another with gladness. As Christians, we have a right to eat from the tree of life. In the paradise of God, we will all rejoice and everything will be in perfect order. Be thankful for the gift of God. Dance like David danced in the presence of the King. Remember, secrets can over-burden you and God judges secrets through Jesus Christ.

Chapter 15: The Power of Prayer
HE WHO HAS EARS LET HIM HEAR:

In these last days, spiritual warfare is on the rise. Satan torments us in different ways. The sheep know the voice of the true **Shepherd**, the **Messiah**. Satan is the enemy, the accuser, the adversary, and the author of confusion. He comes to steal, kill, and destroy. When the enemy torments you, call **Jesus** and the saints for prayer and intercession. Resist the devil and he will flee. Thank **God** for His grace and mercy and for spiritual weapons. Put on your full armor of **God** and stay equipped for battle. The power of prayer and faith moves mountains. Humble yourself and pray. Lift your head to the hills from whence cometh your help. The blood of **Jesus** covers us; He is our **Intercessor**. **God** allows us to go through fires so that He can reveal His power and revelation knowledge. Satan is working overtime; he knows his time on earth is short. **God** is pouring out His **Spirit** and equipping us for victory.

Chapter 16: Salvation
HE WHO HAS EARS LET HIM HEAR:

Jesus saves.

Chapter 17: Revelation
HE WHO HAS EARS LET HIM HEAR:

Read the Bible, the Book of Revelation.

**This book contains my views and does not represent the views of the United States Air Force or United States Government. **

After this manner therefore pray ye: Our Father which art in heaven, Hallowed be thy name. Thy kingdom come, Thy will be done in earth, as it is in heaven. Give us this day our daily bread. And forgive us our debts, as we forgive our debtors. And lead us not into temptation, but deliver us from evil: For thine is the kingdom, and the power, and the glory, for ever. Amen.

Matthew 6:9-13 (KJV)

AUTHOR'S BIOGRAPHY

 I was born third from the youngest of ten siblings in Lorain, Ohio. I moved to the city of Elyria at the tender age of six. My childhood was very memorable and I have no regrets. I'm blessed and highly favored. I dedicate this book to my sister and Angel, Jacqueline Preston who went to be with the Lord "7" years ago on April 21, 2000 (Good Friday). You are my keeper.

I graduated from Elyria High School in 1983 and joined the United States Air Force in 1985. In accordance with God's plan, I've been stationed in North Carolina, Nevada, Virginia, Hawaii, Colorado and Florida. God used me as a vessel to write this book. His mighty hand of protection shelters me from the storms of life.

I'm married to Irwin Noel (my silent strength of fifteen years) who is also in the Air Force. God blessed us with two gifted seeds, Tyrell and Tavaris. I'm excited about the next chapter of my life. I plan to retire in a few years and devote more time to God and my family. Other plans include restoring Mother Helen's house, planting a garden, scrapbooking, publishing poems, playing the piano, picking berries, singing in the choir, fishing, and finishing the family genealogy.

My prayer: "That I may publish with the voice of thanksgiving, and tell of all thy wondrous works." Psalm 26 (KJV)